# What Has Your Sister Done?

Laura Lofgreen

Vintage Bird Press, April 2017

Published in the United States.
www.vintagebirdpress.com

Cover Photo: Betina Workman
Photograph of: Rosa Dilworth Reyes and daughter
Cover design: Jerah Moss

ISBN-13: 978-1545487709

# What Has Your Sister Done?

## STORIES OF UNPLANNED PREGNANCY

LAURA LOFGREEN

Vintage Bird Press

## *Dedication*

To my son Canyon Samuel,
who taught me to love no matter the timing.

# Introduction

*What Has Your Sister Done?* is a collection of true stories about girls and women and their unplanned pregnancy. Some have kept their babies while others placed their babies for adoption or terminated their pregnancies through abortion. Because many aspects of unplanned pregnancy aren't talked about, I'm hoping these stories will open the door and help someone in the same situation. I believe our stories are more powerful than we realize.

To those of you who have contributed to this project, thank you. Every story I've read has changed me in some way. To consider the love, the strength, the loneliness, the uncertainty, the judgment – these stories are the most real things I've ever read. For those of you who have faced unplanned pregnancy, whatever you've done, you are my heroes. Society has not been fair to you. These stories speak truth and show how strong and resilient women are. They demonstrate the strength, fear, social barriers and all the diversity that comes with such an experience. Many have suffered through abuse and speak about such injustices, while others share where they found support. Many stories have both aspects – abuse in some areas and support in others.

Why am I interested in stories of unplanned pregnancy? In my life, I had many lessons to learn from a pregnancy scare in my twenties to an unplanned pregnancy at the age of forty-two. To me, this journey is personal and through my research, I started drawing amazing conclusions. I wrote my own experience in my memoir *Starving Girl* (2016) and the truth set me free. I wanted to offer this healing gift to others. As I became more confident in my goal, more stories came in.

During my senior year of college, I was the assistant director of a narrative project where we collected stories about a diversity of issues and presented them in a theatrical stage performance. I remembered how each story demonstrated a variety of social issues when all we were doing was sharing someone's personal story. In *What Has Your Sister Done*, I offer no analysis, but allow the reader to interpret what's meaningful. Readers are independent thinkers and can come to their own conclusions. Stories on unplanned pregnancy demonstrate certain aspects of societal norms and changes we as a people need to make to better support our sisters. Each story of unplanned pregnancy stands as a witness to what is going on in our society, how each sister stands in an unforeseen place and with a leap of faith, does the best she can. On its own, each story has something important to say. I appreciate these stories and I love my beautiful sisters. From the bottom of my heart, thank you to those who have supported this project.

Working on this book has opened my eyes to many things, but most importantly how much these girls and women need to be validated. These stories need to be shared and although many of them were submitted anonymously, I felt I could see every girl's or women's face in each story. I want people to support them and like me, change their bias towards those facing unplanned pregnancy. This is not just a women's issue, but everyone's issue.

I've read each story countless times and continue to cry like I'm reading them for the first time. I've done this for my baby boy Canyon and my sisters, all my sisters no matter what they chose. I love them both on a level I can't describe. I feel I'll be collecting stories of unplanned pregnancy throughout my life – to validate those who are pushed aside, who may feel like no one cares, because I care. I care.

Table of Contents

In a world of constant shortages and never-enoughs, there's one thing we have an unlimited supply of – our stories.

–Laura Lofgreen

# One
## *"Mommy, I'm Going to Have a Sister."*

I had been separated from my husband for 1 ½ years and was raising our five-year-old daughter Kelsey on my own with minimal support. I was afraid and wondered how was I going to raise her on my own? I had no education, no job and had been a stay-at-home mom up until the day I filed for divorce.

Then there was the game I constantly played in my mind. I felt like I failed my daughter by leaving my husband. Our perfect family unit was shattered. I didn't think I'd have anything going for me if I left my husband, but with him I had no self-esteem. What was wrong with me? Before we met, I was a strong, independent woman with dreams, ambitions and goals. Now, I was weak and vulnerable. I didn't even recognize myself in the mirror. Still, I couldn't give up easily and would do everything possible to keep my family together. It was worth it. Maybe I was just overreacting. If I acted better, kept the house cleaner or was prettier maybe my husband would change. How many times had I tried to convince myself I could put up with his verbal abuse? He didn't really mean to put me down and treat me like I was worthless. Many men used profanity when speaking with a spouse, or at least that's what I tried to tell myself.

I decided to give my husband one last chance and moved back in with him for a few weeks. The first few days were blissful, full of laughter and late-night talks, but by the end of the second week his abusive behavior only worsened. To make matters worse, he was drinking alcohol. His drinking magnified his abusive tendencies. That's when I decided no more. I reluctantly moved back home with my parents, still upset I couldn't afford a place on my own. Kelsey and I shared a bed in my bedroom and I was so grateful to have her to hold on to. She was the best thing in my life. One morning she woke up and said, "Mommy, I had a dream I'm going to have a baby sister." I assured her there was no way that would ever happen. I had never had normal periods, menstruating only once or twice a year. It had been months since I'd been intimate with my husband, but I went ahead and took a pregnancy test. You can imagine my shock when the test read positive. I purchased several more pregnancy tests, one of every brand, and took one after another. Each read positive. It's hard when you're in that situation to understand how you're going to feel in the future, but at that moment, I felt devastated.

I had miscarried a baby a year after Kelsey was born, so it quickly occurred to me there was a chance I would miscarry again. That left me somewhat hopeful. Sure, I thought of abortion, but I was too much in denial to really consider it. And how could I tell my husband? Would he be happy? Would this make a difference in where our divorce was going? I made the phone call and told my husband I was pregnant, reassuring him I didn't want to have another baby with him. I shouldn't have been surprised my husband's response was hurtful. "If you have abortion, I'll be sure to tell our daughter when she's older and she'll resent you." His reaction was a form of control, but I could see right through it.

My mind was in constant turmoil and the pregnancy was all I could think about. Who could I trust? I didn't want to tell anybody. My parents didn't know. They already thought my situation was dire enough. I was around four months along and still didn't think I could keep this baby. I couldn't even take care of myself and Kelsey. Abortion seemed like the responsible thing to do. My cousin had had an abortion. It had been a one-night stand and the guy told her if she didn't get an abortion, her would punch and hit her until she lost the baby. I had watched how it affected her. She suffered with depression and often expressed sorrow and regret over her decision.

On the other hand, Kelsey (the only one I had told other than my husband) was thrilled I was pregnant with her sister (she kept insisting). She had wanted a little sister ever since she started talking. When Kelsey was three-years-old she picked out a name for a baby sister. The name was Kiley. Whenever I thought about getting an abortion, I tried to do what I was taught by the prochoice movement; I tried to think that the baby inside me wasn't really a person, but Kiley, the name my daughter had picked out several years earlier, kept running through my mind.

It was my responsibility to give Kelsey the best life possible. Was giving her a sibling worth it? Was I living in a dream world thinking it could all work out? I hoped the pregnancy would never end. I needed indefinite time to make up my mind. One day it seemed right to keep the baby, while the next day I knew abortion was the only answer. When I was about six months along, I applied for government assistance and went to the doctor. I was told the baby was a girl and what a surprise my baby's due date was the same day Kelsey's had been.

Everyone's situation is different, but I finally took responsibility. I'd had sex and was now pregnant. I believe every woman should make up her own mind, but I also think when you're young, you don't think the decisions you make are going to affect you for the rest of your life. For me, I knew aborting my baby would be something I couldn't live with. I can't tell someone else what they can and cannot do with their body, but for me, this was the only choice I could give myself. It was between me and God. I didn't want to live with regret. I didn't want to tell my daughter I had aborted her sibling. I didn't want to be held accountable for the death of my own child.

Throughout the pregnancy, I felt abandoned by God. When I started showing at six months, the feelings grew worse because people were asking me questions. I started to panic. My divorce was finalized when I was eight months pregnant. I was huge and the consequences of my divorce seemed even more devastating. At the courthouse, I went into the bathroom and just bawled. I later hugged Kelsey. She was a healing agent to me. She was my miracle and best friend.

At this point, I didn't feel connected to the baby growing inside me. I still had regrets and concerns. I was still in denial about what was coming. I didn't think I could love this child as much as Kelsey, but the day did come when I went into labor and delivered a perfect little baby. The minute they put my baby into my arms, I knew I had made the right decision. Instantly, my baby brought me so much joy and peace. When before I felt lonely, I now felt so complete. I was overwhelmed with joy and I did name her Kiley. This perfect baby showed me I can love more than I ever imagined. In all my bad choices I made with my ex-husband, this was the best thing that came out of it. Kelsey, who was also struggling with the divorce being finalized, now feels complete with the sister she always knew she would have. She's so proud of her baby sister and they are as close as close can be. Kelsey has been through more than most six-year-olds. She's seen me in the depth of despair and is my greatest strength.

Now, when Kiley gets hurt, falls down or anything, I think back to when the abortion literature told me my baby was just a fetus. She is a human being, like me or Kelsey.

As much as you think you can't do something, when you are in that situation you are so much stronger than you realize. I am doing this. Kiley is almost one year old. I found a job that lets me take her to work. I am enrolled in school full-time and will graduate in one more semester. My ex-husband pays child support and although it's minimal, we just make it. I just roll with the punches and take life one day at a time with my two beautiful daughters.

— Anonymous

## Two
## *I. Had. An. Abortion.*

I. Had. An. Abortion.

I choke on those words. They get stuck in my throat like a rock. I have only said those words out loud three times since it happened: to my parents when I went through my divorce, knowing it had the potential to come out in court; to my current husband, who listened to me tell him, as he loved and comforted me, and played a huge role in my healing; and to my church leader.

I was sixteen years old, and in a terrible, abusive relationship. I had no self-esteem. I had established a pattern of making poor choices, and as a result, had no self-esteem or self-worth. I must be clear; I was born into a wonderful family. I was raised Christian and experienced a wonderful childhood. My childhood was truly ideal. I had the best parents and family anyone could ever hope for! My parents never uttered an unkind word to each other and never argued. They were, and still are, the most amazing and loving people I know. Over the years, they have helped me see forgiveness and heal.

I take full responsibility for my actions and decisions, and do not want to push blame onto anyone else. I believe my journey to this low point in my life, began when I was in second grade. I was molested by my elementary school teacher. I told no one. I was scared and had internalized it. Looking back, I believe this incident was the catalyst that brought me to where I was at sixteen. After my experience in second grade, and the feelings I hid deep inside of me, my self-worth was tied to how women are viewed and objectified sexually. I felt I was a sexual object. Let me reiterate, this was not what I was taught, nor how I was raised. My father is a perfect gentleman and reveres women. He cherishes my mother, my sister and I. As a doctor, he devoted his career to taking care of women. I truly believe Satan capitalized on me being sexually abused and used it against me as he constantly told me I was worthless and damaged. I continued down a path of promiscuity, as I felt this was all I was good for. I dated a boy who was older and he wore on me about having a sexual relationship. He was manipulative and convincing. I had, in the back of my mind, the thought that this was all I was good for and all men wanted from me, or from women in general. I felt if I wanted to be loved or have a boyfriend I had to give in to their desires. I felt dirty and used. When this relationship ended, I vowed to do and be better. Then, the voice started again, telling me that I wasn't worthy. I wasn't forgiven. Soon, I was back on the path of bad choices, it was a vicious cycle.

I found myself in an abusive relationship when I was sixteen, and soon after, found out I was pregnant. I was terrified. I first turned to my boyfriend. Yes, the same boyfriend who was abusing me. He was controlling and abusive from the beginning of the relationship. He controlled everything I did. He told me not to wear makeup, how to dress, where to go, who I could be friends with, and even what color I could polish my nails. He told me if I ever broke up with him he would kill me. So, when I found myself in this situation, I felt, "No one will understand. No one will listen to you. You will be in big trouble if anyone finds out," etc. My boyfriend said the same things to me, as well like, "You are dumb. I have to think for you. Nobody else will love you." He was not a member of the same faith as me, and made it clear I was also no longer to be a part of that faith. He was the oldest in his family. His entire family were controlling bullies and abusive too. I should have seen the signs. It was the polar opposite of the loving family I had. He told me we couldn't have the baby. He wanted to graduate from high school. His parents would be disappointed. I felt trapped and cornered. I knew his family would make this a horrible situation for my family. He convinced me that abortion was the answer. I knew it was not, but I felt there was no other choice. How could this be happening? I was drowning in my mind. I wanted to die.

My boyfriend had me make the appointment for a Saturday so he could drive me. I made the appointment from a pay phone in front of a gas station using a false name and information. I did not need any parental consent, nor ID to receive a surgical procedure that would end the life of my baby, and could endanger my own.

I met him on Saturday, after telling my parents I was going to hang out with friends at the mall. We drove to the clinic. I prayed the whole way there asking that God would forgive me.

We checked in. It was $285 for this procedure. It smelled awful, I can remember the smell. I wanted to throw up. I wanted to run, looking back, I think I was having an anxiety attack. I was told to take all my clothes off and change into a gown. They had me take a pregnancy test. I prayed it was negative. It was positive. They had me lay on a table. Then I heard the vacuum sound. At that moment, I went numb and I died inside.

The only memory of the ride home was lying down on the back seat crying. I damned myself and my soul to Hell. I told myself there was no way I could be forgiven for what I had just done. I just committed the most heinous act that a mother could commit. I killed my baby. Who does that? I felt there was no forgiveness for me at that point, and I deserved any and every horrible thing this life had to offer. I remember going home and going to bed. I told my mom I was sick. I felt so disconnected and awful that there was no one I could talk to about this. I was harboring a dark disgusting awful secret. I was the worst mother in the world. How did I get here? Satan lied to me. I believed his lies and it had now ruined my life.

I continued to date this boy, continued to endure his control and abuse. I deserved it. I married him right after high school. I convinced myself that this was my penance for the decisions I'd made. I was forever to be tied to this horrible person who treated me the way he did because we created a life and we destroyed it together. We were bound by this awful secret we shared. He told me I needed to "harden my heart" towards my parents, my family and those I loved the most. I tried to convince myself that the religion I was raised in was not true. I endured his abuse for ten long years, and was completely separated from those I loved and the religion I loved.

To this day, I wonder to myself how old my baby would be and what would he or she look like? Did he or she get a chance to come back and receive the body they deserved, or was that the only chance and I ruined it? I was trapped in this abusive marriage. His threats, verbal, physical, emotional, and sexual abuse continued throughout our marriage. He threatened to kill me if I ever left him, and after we had our two other children, he told me if I left he would kill all of us, or that if I left him I could never take my children with me. So, I stayed. He told me he would tell my parents the truth about me, and all the horrible secrets he knew about me. He told me my parents would never understand, and hated me. More threats and lies. I had not one shred, sliver or ounce of self-esteem left.

My life changed after being married for six years. My brother died. He committed suicide. He never left a note, but did write my name in a notebook, along with the words, "Come back to what you know is true." This was a turning point. I started talking to one of my brother's friends, who happened to be a police officer. He started building me up and repairing my broken soul. He told me my parents would love and help me. He explained to me I was in an abusive relationship and it was called domestic violence. My husband told me daily I was stupid or retarded, and that he had to think for me. I thought I was trapped, with no way out. Satan convinced me I was living an eternal sentence as a result of my decisions.

The day finally arrived that I knew I had to get out of this situation. I realized my children were going to grow up and likely be abused or abuse others. I was downstairs in my child's bedroom, and dropped to my knees and prayed for the first time in a LONG time. I asked God if this was the course I should take. I asked Him for help and to show me the way. Learning about domestic violence and the resources and options available to me, from my brother's friend, gave me knowledge and confidence. Since he knew my family and parents, he gave me courage that I could indeed go to my parents and they would love me, help me and listen.

I found the courage to tell my parents the truth and that I wanted out of my abusive marriage. They did not like my husband and never really did, but they loved me and trusted me to make good decisions for myself. They knew he was abusive, but had no idea to what degree. It's funny, my brother that died, hated him, and knew he was bad news! I know he was helping me out of this situation from where he was in heaven.

One night, I told my husband I was leaving him. Just as he threatened, he went into the closet and retrieved his gun. He pointed it at me and told me he would kill me before he would ever let me leave him and take his children. I put my hand on the gun to stop him and we scuffled for a minute. Then, he just stopped, put the gun on the bathroom vanity, walked into our kitchen, took all of the car keys and left. I went downstairs and started crying. I was terrified he was going to come back, and kill me and the children. About an hour went by, and I heard knocking on my door and the doorbell ringing. I was scared to go to the door. I thought it was his parents, who were crazy like he was! Then I heard my angel mother calling my name. It was my mom and dad. My husband had gone to their house, and told them how horrible I was and how everything was my fault. My parents felt my safety was in jeopardy. As soon as he left, they raced to be with me and protect me.

This started the long drawn-out process of my divorce. We had been together for twelve long years, ten of them married. My brother's friend gave me advice on what to do in my dangerous situation, leaving a domestic violence abuser with threats of bodily harm and death. Talking with him had been building me up and helped me take back control of my life. Taking control of the steps to get out of this marriage was helping me regain some self-worth. I talked to my parents and confessed everything. They were heartbroken, and so sad I was in that situation, at that age, and that I hadn't come to them. They were so kind and so full of love for me. Over the years, through talking with both my parents, I came back to church. My dad talked with me many hours and told me God was loving and merciful. I developed a relationship with Jesus Christ again. I repented as I felt Godly sorrow for what I had done. I truly had a broken heart. I read everything I could find on the subject of abortion and spiritual healing. I needed to know. I rededicated myself and my life to God.

My current husband and best friend has been amazing. He

is so patient and kind, rebuilding me and my self-worth, loving me and never judging me for what I have done. He tells me I am the epitome of how the atonement works, and I am his hero. I love him so very much for helping restore my life and my faith.

I am still sad and full of regret for what I did. If I could go back in time and change what happened, I would. I am so thankful for the cleansing and enabling power of the atonement of Jesus Christ in my life. I don't know where I would be without it. Even with forgiveness I have bad days, which may be a consequence for my choices, but I do know that the Lord loves me, and I am forgiven. All this, because someone believed in me, and helped me believe in myself. I trust that forgiveness is real, and that it applies even to me. I love the hymn, *I Stand all Amazed*:

> I tremble to know that for me He was crucified,
> That for me, a sinner, He suffered He bled and died…
> I marvel that He would descend from His throne divine
> To rescue a soul so rebellious and proud as mine.
> That He should extend his great love unto such as I,
> Sufficient to own, to redeem and to justify.
>
> I think of His hands pierced and bleeding to pay the debt!
> Such mercy, such love and devotion can I forget?
> No, no I will praised and adore at the mercy seat,
> Until at the glorified throne I kneel at his feet.

Oh it is wonderful that He should care for me enough to die for me!

Oh it is wonderful, wonderful to me!"

—Anonymous

# Three
## *Still Haunted By Abortion*

I'm not a writer so I can't convey the story like I want, but it's a message that should be told. My sister was eighteen and she had her first boyfriend who worked in construction. She didn't know she was pregnant, but thought she had the flu or was sick. She was also asthmatic and used some powerful asthma medications at the time. She went to the ER really sick and they took x-rays before checking if she was pregnant, something they would never do today. She had all kinds of tests. Later, they found she was with baby. The jerk fellow I think threw himself off a ladder to fake injury, then he left town. My sister was eighteen, on medication that could possibly harm the baby, plus the x-rays she had been exposed to. It was the 1970's. Abortion had just become "acceptable." We were torn with what to do, because of the medical issues, and she was not in position to care for a baby. She had an abortion. Even still, so many years later, my younger sister and I tear up thinking about it. We were young. It was a horrendous decision. She celebrates that little life every year and if we could take it back, to do it over she would have that baby no matter what. The pressure from others was incredible. Also being young and not knowing what do made it all that more difficult. Today if I could counsel someone thinking about ending a life with abortion I would tell them NO! My sister is the mother of three grown daughters, married to her best friend for thirty-five years, but she is still haunted by that abortion, as am I.

—Anonymous

## Four
## *A Baby Girl Was Just What I Needed*

I'm lying next to Jenna as I write this. My baby girl has just turned six months old! Where has the time gone?! I love this little girl with all my heart and we share such a sweet connection. It hasn't always been this way though. It pains me to remember how I felt during the first few weeks of my pregnancy with her. So many feelings: I felt ashamed, embarrassed, guilty, scared, anxious, worried, and angry.

I should probably let you know that I was already a mom, a young mom. I got married at eighteen and I had my first baby just before my twentieth birthday. I dropped out of college and became a stay-at-home mom. I felt like others were judging me for rushing into marriage and motherhood. I didn't have any friends going through what I was. I felt so young and alone. But I absolutely loved being a mom! Being a mom was something I had looked forward to ever since I can remember. My first baby was definitely a life adjustment. Just after he turned one, we decided we wanted to try for baby number two. My siblings were my best friends growing up so I wanted my son to have a similar relationship with someone close in age. The day our oldest turned twenty-two months old, we welcomed our second little boy. They brought us so much joy, but SO MUCH WORK. Our oldest wasn't sleeping through the night until after our second was born.

Trying to get through life with little sleep is incredibly difficult and challenging.

My husband and I adored our two boys and decided we were content to wait until our second was about four or five years old to try for another baby. I needed a little more sleep! But plans changed and I ended up pregnant a lot sooner than we had anticipated. This was going to put our second and third babies at twenty-one months apart. I felt terrible. I loved my boys so much and I was afraid I wouldn't be able to mommy them to my full potential because I would have another baby too close in age with them. Plus, I was finally gaining control of my depression. I was afraid a pregnancy and new baby would set me back. And my husband and I were still working through a rough point in our marriage. This "blessing" couldn't have come at a more inconvenient time. There are so many people out there that want babies that would make amazing parents! I didn't need another baby. Not yet anyway.

My husband and I remember the night of the big "oops." My first thought was to take Plan B from the pharmacy. If I did it needed to be soon. But immediately after I had the thought I had an overwhelming prompting that I was going to be pregnant and it was something I needed to carry on with. Even though I knew it was all supposed to happen, it didn't make it any easier. I didn't want her yet! I was finally growing, and life was looking better, I was afraid she would push me back in my personal growth. I wasn't ready to face another challenge. I felt so guilty for not feeling the joy I felt when I found out I was expecting my first two.

The morning I took that pregnancy test I cried and cried off and on for the rest of the day, for a couple of weeks in fact. I had gotten myself into a deeper state of depression. How could I physically care for and love another baby? I could barely handle my boys. The hardest part was announcing we were pregnant. It was a huge relief once everyone knew. I thought I would be judged for being pregnant with my third at the age of twenty-two, and I probably was by some, but who cares?

As my pregnancy progressed I became a little more excited. We found out we were having a baby girl just before Christmas. But towards the end of my pregnancy I realized I hadn't grown to love her as I had my boys. I couldn't even decide on a name! I was worried I wouldn't "connect" with her, but boy was I wrong. The moment I met her I felt the deepest connection between us. It was like I've always known her. My love for her continues to grow daily. And the ironic part is that I've actually adjusted to being a mom of three so much easier than after either of my first two. She was the best newborn, and is such a sweet baby to this day. She actually makes me feel as though I'm doing this parenting thing somewhat right! Whenever I'm going through a rough day or questioning my abilities, the way she looks at me reminds me that I can get through just about anything. We've actually decided we are going to try for our fourth just after she turns a year old. It's incredible how unique and special each child is, and how rewarding they can be!

—Anonymous

## Five
## *I Never Knew Love Until I Met My Son*

My dad sexually abused me from the age of three until the age of thirteen. He would say things like, "The only thing a woman is good for is sex." He would get me drunk and abuse me. If I wanted anything, I either had to let him hit me or sexually abuse me. He was such a womanizer and cheated on my mom with multiple women. I found out later he was also abusing my sister. Because of the abuse from my dad, I had weird emotions mentally. I did everything wrong for me. Anything that I could do that was bad for me, I would do it. I had several sexual partners before the age of 14 and put myself in dangerous situations. I started doing drugs when I was young and I just wanted to die. My parents split up because my sister's friend turned my dad in to the police. The police told my mom she either needed to divorce my dad, or she would lose us kids. I didn't know at the time that was the reason they split up, but that was why Mom moved out.

I became pregnant with my son when I was fifteen. When I found out I was pregnant, my boyfriend wanted me to have an abortion. He was the same age as I was. When I became pregnant I started skipping school. I wasn't knowledgeable of health. I didn't know smoking was bad, even though people told me. I didn't trust anybody, so I did whatever I wanted. My mom took me to the state social services and made me a ward of the court. There was a home for pregnant girls and my mom was embarrassed to be with me. I told my caseworker about the abuse from my dad and I wanted to keep my baby. The entire time, my mom said to the caseworker, "I just knew my daughter would end up pregnant."

I was in a Salvation Army group home and they took me to church. I got my GED and had my son. I was smoking pot and breaking curfew. Right after I had my son, a high school friend felt sorry for me and wanted to marry me. I had moved back in with my mom and she said if I didn't get married she'd try to have my son taken away. I told my high school friend I'd marry him because I didn't want to lose my son. My son was the only thing I had. When I held my boy, I felt so much love from him. The reason I didn't abort him when everybody told me to was because I needed him so much. The minute I found out I was pregnant, I just loved my baby. If I wouldn't have kept my son, I would have ended up dead, I just know it. So, I married this friend of mine. He was an alcoholic and he kept having affairs. We were married for 10 years, but were only together off and on for three years. I had two other children with him, so by the time I was twenty-one I had three kids. I was a heavy drug addict, a mess on everything and suicidal. Men used me for sex. Still, these children were the only love I'd ever known. I spent every free dollar I had on my kids. I did everything I could to support them. They were the only reason I stayed alive. I hated myself so much, the only joy I had was my three boys. I was on welfare until my youngest boy started kindergarten. At that time, I was able to get a job.

Now, I'm fifty-four and I'm religious. I believe the Lord sent my son to me when I was fifteen. All of my sons gave me a greater purpose. Now, I do sidewalk counseling and talk to girls about their unplanned pregnancies. I know God knew us before we were even formed in our mother's womb. This year, I am celebrating my twenty-fifth wedding anniversary with a wonderful man. I love my three sons and have four beautiful grandkids. At my church, I went through a sexual abuse healing class and learned to forgive my dad. I have been transformed.

Before having my son at the age of fifteen, I had no purpose, but my little son, that little boy, was my salvation and then my boys that followed gave me such purpose. The bond of a child is indescribable. Until you actually experience that, you don't know. I'm not a political person, but I hope people choose life and turn to God when they become pregnant.

—Anonymous

## Six
## *Losing the Baby Was Not What I Wanted*

Twenty-four years ago, I found out I was pregnant with my second child. I had recently lost my first child by miscarriage and was not happy to be pregnant again. I was twenty-five and not only was I scared I would lose the baby, but the father, my boyfriend, had been lying and cheating on me. I didn't want to have this man's baby. I was really afraid. Shortly after I found out I was pregnant, I told him and he wanted me to get an abortion.

"No," I shouted. Even though I didn't want to be pregnant, there was no way I was going to terminate. In college, I had done some sidewalk counseling and was actively pro-life. I had taken science classes just so I could learn about fetal development, but once I graduated, I worked full-time, so no longer did I have time to help those with unplanned pregnancies. Now I was the girl experiencing the unplanned pregnancy.

I went to a new doctor and he did an ultrasound. I will never forget when he showed me the baby's heart beating on the screen. I found it absolutely amazing, but from the start of the pregnancy, I was having problems. I was spotting and cramping. I had to quit my job because my doctor put me on bed rest. I never wanted to be pregnant, and now there I was, out of work with a boyfriend who wanted me to abort. It was not a good time. I was depressed and moved back in with my parents. My mother was disappointed, but she was still supportive. I started to feel scared I would lose the baby. Even though I didn't want to be pregnant, I didn't want my baby to die.

From the moment I saw her heart beating, I felt like she was a girl so I named her Rachel. There's a verse in the Bible of Rachel weeping for her children who were no more (Jeremiah 31:15). I was weeping too because of my situation. I was heartbroken my boyfriend wanted this baby dead. I reached out to a pregnancy resource center called *The Nurturing Network* and they helped me find another place to live, but I lost the baby a couple of days before I was to move. I was ten weeks and four days when I lost the baby. I started miscarrying at my boyfriend's house with some heaving bleeding and cramping. I was frightened and in so much pain. My boyfriend wouldn't call an ambulance and said he wouldn't take me to the hospital. I ended up driving myself to the hospital, but didn't make it. I had to pull over at a gas station and told them to call 911. "I'm having a miscarriage," I said. There was a paramedic inside the store and she was a big help. Finally, an ambulance came and took me to the hospital where I had a D&C.

As much as I didn't want to be pregnant, I still miss that baby. You never ever really forget. For a long time, my arms literally ached because I couldn't hold her. I couldn't bury her. I couldn't see her. I don't know how I survived. I didn't want to. I was in the hospital for a couple of days and nobody talked to me about my loss. It took me several weeks to physically recover, but emotionally, I still cry for my baby.

A mother's love is the strongest bond. Even though I felt like "I can't do this, this isn't the right time," I still loved her with all my heart. The love felt natural, even necessary. My boyfriend never came to the hospital and shortly after, we broke up. I want to say to any girl in an unplanned pregnancy even though you're scared and terrified, you can still do the right thing.

When I was twenty-nine, the doctor discovered scar tissue in my uterus and this was what contributed to my first two miscarriages. I had surgery and when I was thirty, I became pregnant again. I did have to stay on bed rest for four and a half months, but finally I had a healthy baby.

I never thought I'd be the girl looking for help, but I was and now when I reach out to others, I feel I can play a special role in helping them realize how precious their baby truly is.

—Anonymous

## Seven
## *I Am a Feminist and I Kept My Baby*

In a half-asleep daze, with my abdomen in knots, I stumbled to the bathroom, fell to my knees, and began throwing up into the toilet. After a few heaves jolted me fully awake, I sensed someone standing behind me. Before I could turn my head to confirm my suspicions, my mother's delicate hands swept past my cheeks and lightly pulled my hair out of my face.

In that moment I felt like a little girl again – cared for, watched over.

No matter how bad things were growing up, my mother always gave me as much unconditional love as any two parents combined. Oftentimes, our unshakeable familial love was all we had.

She helped me up to the sink. As I began rinsing my mouth, she eyed my midsection as if expecting to see something. I rolled my eyes and assured her it was just a bug, probably something I ate the night before. "I am not pregnant!" I said.

In my mind though, I knew she wasn't the only one I was trying to convince. I was only sixteen, and my on-again, off-again boyfriend had started using drugs again – this time more than just recreationally. As I stared into the sink, my hand nervously jostling the toothbrush around my mouth, my mother disappeared.

I wanted nothing more than to shut down my brain and push these anxieties as far out of my mind as possible. I climbed back into the reassuring comfort of my warm bed. As my eyes grew heavy, the hum of my fan lulled me back to sleep.

What must have been hours later, since the sun was shining through my window, my mother walked back into my room and gently placed her hand on my arm. "I need you to get up and pee," she said. What? When did I suddenly become a toddler again, in need of reminders for this sort of thing? That's when I rubbed my eyes open and noticed the Dixie cup and tiny white stick resting in the palm of her hand.

Immediately, my heart plunged down to the base of my spine. No! Was this really happening? I reassured myself that there was nothing to discover, and so with the last sliver of blissful ignorance I would ever have, I scooped up the cup and did as I was told.

When I returned from the bathroom, I handed over the paper cup and I found my way back to the warmth of my bed. I could only see the lower half of my mother's body as she leaned over the sink. And just as my head rediscovered the pillow I saw her rock back on her heels, letting out a slow and steady sigh. Surely, she couldn't tell anything yet.

"How long do those things normally take?" I asked.

"Three and a half minutes," she replied.

But before I could relish my relief, she finished, "But it only took 30 seconds."

And then, my world imploded.

As I wailed into my mother's embrace, all I wanted was to rip my stomach out of my body, or better yet leave my body behind all together, for someone else to deal with.

How could I have done this? I knew better. I knew better.

I knew the damage being a single teenage mother would do to a child, because I was that child. My mother was only nineteen when she became pregnant with me. She was a sophomore at the University of Texas with such a bright future ahead of her when I came along. Because of me, our lives were racked with hardships. Was I prepared to put an innocent child through that, seeing as I was little more than a child myself?

The following days were a blur, and so many choices lay ahead of me. Being single and sixteen, it seemed only logical to have an abortion – at least to other people. Every time someone suggested it, though, I would flinch. Didn't they realize all of the reasons they were giving that I should abort were the very same reasons my mother should have had an abortion? Didn't they realize every time they said I'd be better off without this baby, they were saying the world would be better off without me?

I was spared from death and, while life hadn't always been perfect, it was much better than the alternative. Who was I to take the life of this child, brought into the world by no fault of his own? I felt like I would have been a coward to make such a choice. And if my mother had taught me anything, it was how to be strong. No matter how many times life kicked us down, we got right back up.

This was no different. I wasn't going to let the world tell

me how weak I was, how this precious child was going to ruin me, how miserable we would be because of our circumstances. I knew since my mother was strong enough to choose me, I was strong enough to choose him.

Thirteen years later I look back on that time and I see how much I've grown, how much this child has changed me for the better. It's hard to remember that day's fear and the panic now. The only time I feel those emotions is when I realize how easy it would have been to buy into the lie the doubters told me and lose my child forever.

I panic when I imagine my life without this kid.

I feel scared for women going through crisis pregnancies with less support than I had. My heart breaks for the girls who choose abortion because, rather than believing they are strong enough, they're told, "You can't."

If you want to know where the stigma surrounding abortion comes from, it is from pregnant women being told they are not good enough, strong enough, or woman enough to be a mother. It's not the pressure society puts on women to carry children in less than desirable circumstances; it's the fact that they know when they make the choice to abort they are accepting defeat. They are denying the biological awesomeness their bodies are capable of, and the inherent strength they have to turn "a mistake" into the best thing that will ever happen to them.

So, until you find a way to rid us of the sense of our own feminine strength, you will never be able to remove the stigma of abortion, which denies it.

Oh, and as you can probably see, not all abortion stories have to end in abortion, some can end like this.

—Used with permission from Destiny Herndon-DeLaRosa.

## Eight
## *Trusting I Knew What Was Best For My Baby*

When I was fifteen I had a boyfriend named Brian. We were seeing each other and ended up having sex. Around the time I was sixteen, his mom came to me and said, "Brian thinks you are pregnant." I couldn't believe it. His mom offered to take me to the doctor and that's how I found out I was pregnant. My boyfriend later said he purposely got me pregnant because he knew I had wanted to break up with him. To say I felt betrayed is an understatement. I was young and wanted to finish high school. I went to my church leader and told him I was pregnant. I then told him I would only tell my parents I was pregnant if he was there. It took every ounce of courage to tell my parents and honestly, they took it better than I thought.

My boyfriend had been abusive to me and I'd talked about leaving him. The first thing my mom said when I told her I was pregnant was, "You know, you don't have to marry him." My boyfriend had been in juvenile jail off and on and he was involved in a lot of bad things. I definitely didn't want to marry him.

I went to my church's social service for counsel and for the first five or six months, I thought I was going to keep the baby. I would be just a month shy of graduation when he was born, so I knew I could do it. But the social service agent gave me a paper that had the pros and cons of keeping my baby versus adoption. I realized all the reasons I wanted to keep my baby were for me, but placing him for adoption was what was best for him. My boyfriend's older brother had two children out of wedlock and I watched him and his girlfriend struggle, even sometimes fight and do all that they could to make ends meet. That's when I realized I couldn't keep my baby. I couldn't do that to him. I wanted to keep him for selfish reasons, because I didn't want to be without him, but he deserved more. I made the decision to place him for adoption. From that moment forward, I carried him knowing I was carrying him for someone else. As hard as it was, the minute I made my decision I felt a lot of peace.

At that time, adoptions were closed, so I knew I couldn't have any contact with my baby once I placed him. I read about three families I could choose from. One of the families I knew without a doubt was the right family. My boyfriend had to sign off on the adoption, but he was adamantly against it. Finally, his parents talked him into it and he also agreed on placing our baby with this particular family. When I went in to sign the papers for the adoption, the social service counselors said they felt like a different family was better for our baby. I just about lost it. All of a sudden I doubted everything. Was I making the right decision? If I couldn't trust my intuition, then what did I have? My mom was upset and said to the agent, "How dare you do this just as she's about to sign the papers?" My mom encouraged me to believe in my decision. I knew the family I'd originally picked was right. I had prayed about it and this was what I wanted for my baby. The social service agency respected my position and signed an affidavit that the baby would go the family I had picked.

Near my due date, I went into to labor and told my doctor I wanted no epidural. I wanted to feel everything in that moment. I wanted to feel everything of him, my beautiful baby boy, for very soon after he would be gone. When he was born, I didn't get to spend much time with him because I didn't want to get too attached. I named him Michael. After he was born, he was taken away to his new family.

Several months later, I went into the social services for some follow-up and there was no one in the front office. I looked through some files and found the paperwork on the family that adopted my baby. I think I just had to know that he was safe with the family I'd picked. I looked in it and there were the parents' names. I never tried to contact him or them. Per the adoption agreement, I was able to send letters the first five years and they sent me pictures that first year. When Michael turned seventeen, I found him and his parents on Facebook. I contacted his parents and told them who I was. What's funny is they had done their own investigation. They knew the area I lived in and they knew who I was the whole time too. It was like we'd been friends all along. They told me when Michael was a baby, the social services informed them I knew who they were and had warned them I might try to contact them. Michael's family knew everything would be alright. In a quiet conversation, Michael's adoptive mother later told me, "During the time you were deciding if you would place Michael for adoption, I had an overwhelming feeling that I had a baby coming my way. I was told I needed to pray for you, to help you have strength."

My son is twenty-four years old now. He is such an incredible person. He has an older sister whom his parents adopted too. They are amazing. They come to family things and I love them so much. I wouldn't have it any different, even though it's been so hard. At times, it feels like the death of a child. I gave birth to someone I love so much, but he was gone from my life. I lost a son, but gained the truth that I did what was best for him. Michael and I have been able to get to know each other and I explained to him why I placed him. His parents saved all the letters I wrote him and as an adult, he was able to read them. He told me, "Those were the hardest letters I've ever had to read." He thanked me and said he understood why I had to place him for adoption. That meant so much. Even though I gave him to another family, I always wanted him. I always felt like someone was missing. He knows that he was wanted by me so much. He knows I wanted him to have a good life. I wasn't able to provide him with what he deserved. He went to college, he does computer software work and is so handsome. He looks like his dad, but acts so much like me. Even though I didn't raise him, his personality is so much like mine. When he was fourteen, he suffered with depression. When his adopted mom told me that, my heart broke. I had suffered with depression and so had his dad and I'm so thankful his parents helped Michael work things out.

I got pregnant later at eighteen and had a daughter. I was

with a different guy and the circumstances were different. I was so happy that this time, she was mine. I mourned the loss of my son and my daughter didn't take his place, but I was so happy I could keep her. I kept Michael's adoption quiet until my oldest daughter was sixteen. My kids were shocked when I told them. I kept a memory book about Michael and had it in my closet for years. After the initial shock wore off, my kids were so excited about having an older brother and they loved looking through the book.

Placing my baby for adoption was the hardest thing I'd ever done. My mom wanted to ship me off to California, but I said, "No, I won't hide." I went to school my entire senior year pregnant. I was called slut and other names, but I'm no better or worse than anybody else. I had a teacher that called me after I gave birth to my son and he asked how the baby was. When I told him I placed the baby with another family, the teacher's tone changed and it was like he was disgusted with me. There's this stigma that placing your baby for adoption means you don't want your baby. Nothing could be further from the truth.

Now, I'm a grandma and my little granddaughter looks like a baby I've seen over and over again in my dreams. To have the chance to love on her is one of the most amazing experiences ever. A baby brings such a gift into a home.

If you are pregnant, I would say listen to your gut. My intuition has never steered me wrong. Do what you think is best. Don't doubt yourself on that. I doubted myself so many times when I was pregnant, even when I signed the papers, but as the mother of my child, I knew what was best for him. I never considered abortion because I knew he deserved to live. I didn't have the right to tell him he didn't get to live. He deserved a life. I developed very thick skin because of what I've been through, but I know who I am. I've withstood other people's judgment of me, but I could do that because I know I'm a daughter of God. I'm just as valued as they are.

—Anonymous

# Nine
## *Regret — One Sister's Story*

This story would remain untold, if it weren't for the courage of my friend, Laura Lofgreen, a sweet mother and talented author. She has publicly shared her experience with sexual abuse as a teenager. I experienced similar abuse. Many times I was sexually abused as a young child. A couple of times it happened on dates as a teenager. I think abuse and abortion are connected. Abortion, it seems to me, is an extension of abuse that turns inward, against the self. However, it goes deeper than the self. I wish I could stop the feeling of regret.

I was fifteen years old, nearly twenty-eight years ago, when I realized I was late. It scared me to the core because I thought I couldn't be pregnant! Then, my parents would know, everyone would know that my boyfriend and I had sex. He already had the reputation for being "that kind of guy." He wasn't religious at all. He was physically abusive, but, worst of all, he was emotionally, verbally, and psychologically abusive and sarcasm was a tool he used against me regularly. There was a night when he found out I had talked to an old boyfriend at school, so he forced me to have sex. Since I had consented before, I figured there was nothing I could do about it. I felt so isolated and every step I took was done in secrecy and shame. I told a friend that I was late and said she would drive me to Planned Parenthood because it was close to her neighborhood. I was fifteen, so I didn't even have a license to drive! I'll never forget receiving the results from a total stranger who confirmed I had become pregnant. I cried all day and stayed at my friend's house that night. There wasn't a chance I'd tell my mom, we didn't have a close relationship at all, and she wasn't healthy in the least, so I couldn't talk to her. Another startling fact was that I overheard my mom talking to her friends about unwed mothers and, in her opinion, a pregnant teen should be "sent away" so no one would know about it. I thought that sounded awful. My sister was dating someone who she spent all her time with, so she was unavailable. We also had company staying with us, so my dad was occupied.

I told my boyfriend the results and he said, "It's half mine! You have to get an abortion because it's not the right time to have a baby. Or, I will take it away..." Did I mention we had an age difference? He was already nearly nineteen years old and graduated from high school. It's really painful to remember how he spoke to me. It was like complete terror. He really thought he had complete control of me and I believed him. His brother had also been part of an "unplanned pregnancy" and his brother's girlfriend got an abortion. I felt like I was worth nothing. I didn't feel like I had any choice in the matter. It makes it particularly difficult when I hear current news about policies on abortion and women marching for "choice." I looked up "choice" and I found that it means when there are many options, many alternatives, a person may select the best option. It didn't feel like a choice at all, it felt like it shouldn't even be an option in the first place for anyone!

As a fifteen-year-old girl, I was allowed to make this life-altering choice completely alone. I had nightmares about baby skeletons (sorry it's so graphic) and could hardly sleep before the abortion. The same friend that took me to Planned Parenthood also gave me a ride to the clinic. My boyfriend was going to pick me up afterwards because he already had a great job post-graduation from high school. I picked out something to wear, it was a Mickey Mouse t-shirt! I always consider this detail as ironic in such a tragic outcome. I seriously didn't know any better. I arrived and sat in a crowded waiting area. There were other women there and I assumed they had appointments for other gynecological care. I was so wrong. We all got ushered into a room to talk to a member of the staff as a cozy group. The staff member asked some key questions: "Has anyone forced you to be here, or pressured you to make this medical decision?" At this point, I wanted to say, "YES! My boyfriend said it was half his and I HAD TO!" Yet, looking at a group of about six other women, I didn't dare say anything —I just kept silent. Then, she asked if we would each take a drug, it was Valium. It didn't have any affect on me whatsoever. I felt just as scared as when I arrived at the clinic.

I don't remember how long I waited until it was my turn. I walked in and saw blood on the floor. It was 1989 and with all the advances in medicine and safety measures about spread of disease such as HIV, it felt like a defiled room. I just remember a lady held my hand, she seemed kind, but the doctor was quick to do his work and it hurt a lot. It hurt more afterwards though. I can't even explain how distorted my whole being felt. It was like a nightmare that started and got stronger and stronger. I saw my boyfriend in the waiting room after a couple of hours and it was all I could do to try to manage the pain. None of the staff workers were attentive to me, it was like I was dirt on the floor and I just wanted to die. I didn't feel any connection to anyone. I wish I hadn't gone there. I didn't feel like a person, I felt like I was chained there. I recovered alone for most of the night in a hotel room. Until I thought of my friend from church... she was much older and could drive to the hotel to see me. I called her and she came right over to see me. I think I finally fell asleep, but, there was no relief. I went back to normal activities right away. It's not like anyone would have helped me, 'cause it was a secret. I'm grateful I healed, physically, that is. Emotionally, I just spiraled down into more despair and I just tried to forget...and kept trying to forget. I tried to do better.

I received a beautiful prayer from a trusted church leader a few years later, at nearly eighteen years of age. Within the blessing I was promised that a family would bud within me and bring ecstasy and joy like I'd never known possible. IT WAS TRUE! I worried that God wouldn't trust me enough to send innocent babies with eternal spirits to my life again. I had three children, then experienced a miscarriage (it was very painful physically and emotionally, as I thought I deserved to have a loss due to the abortion). I had one more beautiful baby after a couple years of mourning the loss of that lost baby from the miscarriage. Each birth experience helped me heal a little more. I had doctors, midwives, doulas (labor support—amazing!), and friends to support me and bring more of God's love into my life! I am so thankful for that divine support.

Years later, I would realize that the beauty of womanhood and motherhood wasn't taken away from me, or damaged. It was dishonored that tragic day in my life. Yet, it didn't take away my desire to create a life within. I think too many women have stopped listening to their own deep longing to be a co-creator with heaven and bring souls to earth. Now, if I may be so bold, using my experiences, I want to SHOUT to all women: THERE IS NO CHOICE IN ABORTION! It is a last resort, it is an act of desperation, and it is a temporary solution that carries weight that lasts too long. I remember the other women there that day. They were all UNHAPPY! They were older women and they mistakenly believed lies that would not allow them to have a baby. The plot of Planned Parenthood is to eliminate unwanted births to prevent those that are deemed lesser than the elite from having babies. If we all felt we had worth, even if money is scarce, even if friends are few, even if life has been hurtful, then the belief would prevail that there is ALWAYS A CHOICE and women can support one another to choose a higher choice. My greatest regret ended up being that I didn't use my voice to say, "No. This isn't the choice I want to live with for another eighty years, or to pass on for my generations to come. It is too heavy for me to carry at my young age and I need help." A woman has power in her choice, don't let it be devalued, or given away, not for any reason, especially not out of fear, loneliness, or lies!

I am sharing this story now, twenty-eight years later, because maybe there is someone who will choose to rise above the present strife and be stronger than I was, choosing the experience that will support their greatest worth and choose better than I did, then this story is worth sharing. In the end, my story reminds me of how completely and powerfully women can stand together for support, love, and truth to create a better world! Best wishes in your choice!

Life is Choice.

—Anonomyous

## Ten
## *The Beginning of My Life*

I've only been dating a few months. We have a lot in common. We both love to sing and play instruments. We have been spending a lot of time together, and decided to take a trip to California. I had the best time with him. I think I'm in love with him oh, it just makes me feel so good about myself and our relationship. We spent way too much time in the sun and I developed blisters all over my back and shoulders. Yes, we have been sexually active but we have been a little careful so I'm hoping everything will be alright. When we got back into town I was not feeling too well and I assumed it was because of the sun exposure. We slept on the ground that night because we were both in pain. The next few days passed and I wasn't feeling any better, just really nauseous. As the days went by I realized that my period hadn't come either. I know exactly what that means and I knew that I needed to take a pregnancy test. I told Peter what was going on and he said it's probably nothing, but we went to the store after all and got a pregnancy test. We took it back to his house and waited 5 minutes for the rest of our lives to be shown to us. The test came back positive. I was pregnant. I have always loved kids and I've always wanted a child of my own so this was very exciting for me, yet I was afraid of how Peter might feel. I have grown up around pregnancies before marriage in my family, but he hasn't so I figured we would handle it differently.

We had to take a couple other pregnancy tests just to make sure that we were seeing things correctly. Each one came out positive. We had to decide how we were going to tell our families, which was probably the hardest part, but we did the best we could. Some handled it very well and some handled it a little harsher than we expected. It was never a question in my mind that I would keep this baby. This baby was mine, ours, our own flesh and blood. Others gave us options like putting the baby up for adoption. I considered it for a short time, but could never wrap my mind around it.

This was our baby and I wanted to be there for every smile, ever step, every failing. We decided to keep him, yes we found out it was a boy! We were so excited. We love each other and decided to get married. I can't say everyone else was as thrilled. People told us right and left that we would fail. What an awful way to start a family, so many loved ones not showing faith in us.

We planned our wedding in six weeks and had our baby boy in March. He has been nothing short of a miracle in our lives. He will always be a part of the beginning of my life and will always be close to my heart.

—Emily Stapley

# Eleven
## *Miracles Unfolded*

My story starts when I became pregnant at seventeen, just before my senior year. My boyfriend and I had been dating for four years and when I told him I was pregnant, he said, "I'm really happy. I always knew we were going to be together." His reaction made me feel like everything was going to be alright.

When I told my parents I was pregnant, my mom reacted with shock, but my dad, who is very action-oriented wanted to know what my plan was. I told him I was scared and that I knew I had disappointed him and my mom. I was the youngest of eleven and as the baby of the family, my parents were very protective of me. He did something I'll never forget. He called me over to the couch and hugged me. "I'll always love you. You'll always be my princess," he said. I'm not sure how long I sat on that couch in his arms, but it meant everything to me.

My boyfriend and I got engaged, but shortly after I found out he was cheating on me. He was a narcissist and made me feel like everything was my fault. Because of me everything had gone wrong. It was my fault I was pregnant, it was my fault he was cheating on me, it was my fault my child wouldn't grow up in happy home. We broke off the engagement and I was shattered. I had been completely dependent and didn't know how I was going to live without him. If the man I was having a baby with didn't want me, who ever would? I was done and decided I was going to take my own life. I drove to a lake and wanted to drown myself. The only reason I didn't do it was because of my baby. I had the thought, *I don't believe in abortion, but killing myself will kill the baby. Committing suicide is like having an abortion.* I knew I had to live long enough to have my baby. If it wasn't for the baby, I would have taken my life that day. I felt like I'd ruined my life, my parents' life, and my friends didn't think I was a good person anymore. When I came home that night, my mom and dad were waiting for me in the living room and were worried sick. I again went to my dad and he held me as long as I needed. He was a silent pull of love. He didn't say a lot, but when he said something, it was so meaningful. His strength lifted both me and my mom. Even still, my mom snapped. She couldn't handle it and worried night and day about me and the baby.

I dropped out of high school and was beyond depressed. I spent three days in my basement and still didn't know what I was going to do with my life. The truth was unplanned pregnancy was not a new thing in my family. My older sister had been pregnant her senior year and my brother's girlfriend became pregnant her senior year. My other sister Collette who lived in Washington called to see how I was doing. My mom suggested I should go up to visit her. I didn't want to leave my basement, let alone my hometown of Bear Lake, Idaho, but my mom felt it would help get me out of my depression. I didn't have the best attitude and was skeptical it would change anything, but decided it was better than where I was at. Once I arrived in Washington my sister suggested we visit the local high school. I was told all my credits would transfer and in order to graduate I would only need another one-half credit, plus a required senior project. This was great news.

My ex-boyfriend would call and he was very emotionally abusive. He would speak with such affection, only to later tell me how awful I was. The tug and pull was taking its toll on me.

My sister introduced me to many of her friends. Surprisingly, I met people who had placed their babies for adoption and many people who had adopted their children. The irony was a bit much, as I was adamantly against placing my baby for adoption. Only I could love her how she deserved to be loved.

In order to graduate, I decided to do my senior project on teenage pregnancy. I needed to interview all sorts of people including people who'd been pregnant and had their baby while in high school, people who'd aborted and people who placed their baby for adoption. My rose-colored glasses came off and I could see how keeping my baby, who I now knew was a girl, wouldn't be the best for her. She would either be taken care of by my parents or in daycare because I would be working forty-plus hours a week to support us. I wanted her to have dance lessons, something I'd never had as a kid. I would start dating again and I was afraid that she would get attached or that perhaps some of the men I dated wouldn't treat her well. As my pregnancy progressed, my eyes opened up to how awful my ex-boyfriend had treated me. It was horrifying to consider he would try to father our daughter. There was no way I would let him treat her how he treated me. I had felt disposable and I didn't want her to feel that way too. Because of my senior project, my eyes opened up to what adoption could offer my baby.

I was about five months along when I realized adoption was the right option for me. I started looking at family profiles and found a family that lived in Arizona. They had been trying to adopt for eleven years. At that same time, I had a cousin who very much wanted me to place my baby with her. She was very adamant that my baby belonged to her, but I didn't feel that was the right thing for my baby. I talked to the family in Arizona and felt good about working with them. In 2010, there was no legal writing in the adoption paperwork that allowed for open adoption. At my request, the parents in Arizona agreed to do an open adoption, something we would work out as I got closer to my due date. One day my adoption counselor talked to their counselor and he confessed the parents had been lying to me about having an open adoption. They didn't want an open adoption and were not going to have that be a part out of our adoption contract. I was devastated beyond belief and felt completely betrayed.

A few days later, I received a letter from my cousin. I felt she was bribing me for my baby. She offered me thousands of dollars so I could go to college, money for my ex-boyfriend to sign away his rights and other financial gifts. This made me feel like my baby was a bargaining tool and I was sick of being manipulated. I told my mom, "I will not place my baby with any of these people. I'm keeping her."

But then, everything changed.

There was a family in Collette's neighborhood that I had been drawn to from the very start. From the moment I met Kim she helped me with my homework and would cook delicious food for me. Kim and her husband Nick had a four-year-old daughter named Lucy, but they weren't able to have any more kids. Kim never brought up adopting my baby, but when everything fell through with the other families, my sister cautiously approached me. She asked if I'd consider allowing Kim to adopt my baby. It was like a light bulb went off and I knew for certain she would be the mother of my baby. I instantly felt like it was right. The next day, I went to Kim's home and asked, "So, what would you think if I asked you to adopt my baby?" She started crying, "Are you serious?" She told me she was adopted and her adoptive mom died when she was nine. She found her birth mom when she was twenty-one. Her birth mom, named Betty, became a big part of her life, not as a mother figure, but as a really good friend. Kim confessed that she and Nick had wanted another baby, but were discouraged to adopt because of how difficult the process was. They had decided months earlier to do foster care and were just a day away from submitting their paperwork!

I was very close to Kim's daughter, Lucy. She was absolutely darling. I watched how Kim mothered Lucy, and even how she mothered me. She treated us both like princesses. Every night she would talk to my baby belly. The baby would react by jumping around and being active in my belly. Kim rubbed my belly and the baby just loved it. It was the cutest thing.

During this time, I was still communicating with my ex-boyfriend and he agreed to sign the adoption papers. He was basically homeless with no car, no job, and no diploma and was bouncing around from friend's house to friend's house. He was also adopted and his adoptive mom knew he was in no place to be a father. She was trying to get him to sign the adoption papers too. I found out while I had been in Washington, he had slept with multiple women. My other sister who lived in Idaho started calling him, encouraging him to sign the adoption papers. She would make arrangements to meet with him and he would never show up. It got to the point where my sister was trying to track him down from one friend's house to another. I finally got on the phone with him and it was one of the only times I'd ever stood up to him. I said, "You either sign the adoption papers, or I'm coming back to raise our daughter and you are paying child support for the next eighteen years." I knew he had two warrants out for his arrest, so I promised him he would never see his daughter. He finally signed.

A few weeks before my due date, I got word he wanted to take his signature back. In Washington, the signature on adoption paperwork did not become valid until forty-eight hours after the birth of the baby. I went to my doctor at thirty-eight weeks and said, "I need to have this baby now before my ex-boyfriend revokes his signature." The doctor did some tests and concluded there was medical need for me to be induced. I was admitted to the hospital and they started the induction. During the second round of the labor-inducing drug Pitocin, my sister called and said, "Your ex-boyfriend is coming up to Washington to take the baby." My blood pressure dropped and the stress was too much. I was showing signs I could have a stroke. My doctor decided to either do an emergency C-section or knock me out with drugs. I remember my feet feeling really hot. I passed out and they were able to safely deliver the baby. I found out later because of a little "help," from my siblings back home, my ex-boyfriend missed his flight. He didn't have the money to re-book, so he never made it to Washington.

Before I went into labor, I had written a very strict birth plan. In it I wrote I did not want to hold the baby first, but Kim and Nick should. After delivery, I was shown the baby, and then quickly they took her to Kim to do skin-on-skin contact. Several hours later, they brought the baby back to me. I was originally going to name her Sylvia, but I knew Kim should name the baby. It was her right. Our baby was named Sarah and I immediately felt it was perfect. I loved it. I decided to keep Sarah with me for the rest of the day, knowing in the evening she would belong to Kim, Nick and Lucy. All ten of my siblings showed up to support me. They brought gifts, wrote letters and showered me with love. My grandmother died when I was eight years old. She had made these little booties for all of her grandbabies. My mom had the last pair of booties my grandmother had made. They weren't finished, so my mom finished them and gave them to Sarah as a gift from our family. We placed them on her. It was the most amazing thing to have my family there for me like that. With my family and Kim, Nick and Lucy we had beautiful photos together.

When I decided to place my baby for adoption, my counselor had me write a letter to myself, reminding me why I was placing her. Without that letter of commitment, I'm not sure if I would have followed through. My emotions were pulling at my heart and I wasn't sure if I was strong enough to do what I'd set out to do.

I was really struggling and had my family pray with me. *How was I going to do this?* I wondered. My baby was lying next to me on the hospital bed and I was taking in all her beauty. How could I live without her? Something that I can only say was a miracle from God happened when little Lucy came in and climbed up on the hospital bed. I loved Lucy with all my heart and would do anything for her. "Is she really my baby sister?" she asked with such innocence and love. I knew the answer. "Yes, she really is," I told her. Lucy was Sarah's perfect big sister. It's hard to explain, but suddenly I felt a shift. Kim and I looked at each other and we finally knew it was time. We both stood up, I walked my baby to her and we hugged together with that little baby in between us. Afterwards, they all left the room. They were a family.

At this point, I started melting down. I sat next to my mom and cried harder then I'd ever cried. The loss of not having Sarah was unbearable but I felt these arms wrapped around me. I felt like these were the arms of Jesus. I took it all in, and then said out loud, "I need my dad." My parents had only recently moved to Arizona and my dad had started a new job, so he was unable to come for the birth. At that moment, the phone near my hospital bed rang and it was my dad. Together we cried and he told me he was so proud of me. Again, I felt his unyielding love and was edified.

Before I placed my baby with Kim, I was able to meet her birth mother, Betsy. Meeting Betsy manifested that everything was going to be alright. Adoption was a living, breathing experience all around me – from my ex-boyfriend who was adopted to Kim being adopted and now my own personal experience of placing my baby for adoption.

I was able to see Sarah one last time and two days later flew from Washington to Arizona. There, I was able to recover and Kim sent me packages with letters and photographs. I knew placing my baby for adoption was right, but I was just living to get through hour by hour. I knew God would make everything ok, but change wasn't happening fast enough. I wanted to feel better. I needed to feel better. It was then that I started receiving letters from total strangers in Washington who had heard of my adoption story. They were encouraging and told me I was an example to them.

My ex-boyfriend tried again to get back with me, but I found out he got another girl pregnant. I changed my phone number. I received hate e-mails from his friends. His friends called me a slut and were making derogatory sexual comments about me. I received several more texts from him that year, but ignored them. I tried to get my life moving again and started dating a guy who actually turned out to be even worse then my ex. This time I was physically and emotionally abused. I broke up with him in my front yard in the middle of the day with my parents watching from the window. I was so afraid of him. Why were all the men I dated so dysfunctional with only their interests in mind? At times, it felt hopeless, but in the back of my mind I had to be better. I had a daughter now and I needed to be my best self because of the love I had for her.

In the meantime, Kim and I both struggled just being away from each other. We'd become best friends. To all of a sudden not have that connection every day was very difficult. I didn't know anybody in Arizona. Even though it was hard, it was the best thing that could have ever happened because I had a fresh start. I could be who I wanted to be, which was the best person for my daughter. She needed to know I was going to make my life right. I started going back to church and met some great women who took me in. I met a friend named Scott and he seemed to see past my tough facade into how I was really feeling. He would show up at my house and say, "I just felt like you were having a bad day." I would open up and share my feelings with him. He introduced me to so many wonderful people, friends I am still close to. I wasn't judged for anything I'd done, they just loved me.

I discovered foot zoning about two weeks after I had Sarah. I had been fighting depression and was struggling with not having her in my life. I went into my first session and when the area on my foot that represented my uterus was rubbed, I felt movement in my abdomen. I wasn't healing as quickly as I'd hoped. The practitioner asked, "Did you just have a baby?" I told him yes.

"You didn't keep her, did you?" he said. By manipulating my feet, he seemed to know I was without my baby.

To be introduced to foot zoning turned my entire life around. I started finding deep healing, not just for placing my daughter, but from my traumatic childhood. As a girl, I was sexually abused from multiple people. My family moved several times during these years and if it wasn't one person who was abusing me, it was someone else. I never told anybody until finally, I'd trusted in and told my ex-boyfriend. This made me even more emotionally dependent on him. In high school, I had a lot of trauma happen. Not just my emotionally abusive boyfriend, but more. In two and half years, I had many people in my life die. My best friend drowned, my uncle was hit on his bike by a drunk driver, my sister's school friend, her little sister and three-month-old baby died in a car accident. These experiences left me hopeless and I didn't feel any value in life. I didn't care what happened to me. Looking back, I can see how my ex-boyfriend manipulated these experiences. I was so desperate for answers, for support and compassion. He took advantage of the rough situation I was in and used me to his advantage.

On Sarah's first birthday, Kim and Nick flew me up to Washington. I was able to see Lucy and Betty again too. We had another set of beautiful pictures taken at Sarah's birthday party.

I started attracting better men into my life. I dated a good man and although he had different life standards then I had, he treated me like a princess. For the first time, I knew I could be with a good man. The relationship didn't work out, but many positive opportunities were coming my way. I was scheduled to move to Germany in a week when I met a really nice guy named Mark. He asked me on a date and I was like, "I'll go for the free dinner." I had dated a couple of Christian boys before Mark and they were *not* alright I'd placed a baby for adoption. The night I met Mark, he had overheard me talking with friends about my daughter. On our first date, he very kindly, with no judgment said, "Tell me about your daughter." When I told him I'd placed her for adoption, he said he was proud of me for making that choice. We talked for several hours and at the end of the date, he said, "I don't think you should move to Germany." He wanted to start dating and confessed the obvious, "If you move to Germany, we can't date."

While praying at my church, an older lady with gray hair came up to me. I told her everything about my baby, Sarah, Kim, my ex-boyfriend and this incredible new guy I met named Mark. She said "Do you want my opinion or do you just want me to listen?" I wanted to hear what she thought and she suggested I not go to Germany, stay in Arizona and give Mark a chance. Mark and I were engaged within a month.

In 2013, I married Mark, the sweetest most stunning man I'd never met. Kim, Nick, Lucy and Sarah attended my wedding. Sarah and Lucy were two of my flower girls. Nine months later I had my son, our little honeymoon baby and I was thrilled to hold a baby I was able to keep as my own. When he was one year old, my best friend called me and said she was pregnant. She wasn't in a place where she could take care of a baby, so we talked about adoption. She knew my story and I asked, "Would you ever consider asking Kim and Nick if they would adopt your baby?" She was thrilled and when her baby was born, she placed him with Kim and Nick. Now, my best friend's son is my daughter's brother. God works miracles.

I don't think many people understand how amazing and necessary adoption is. A person on my facebook even last month made a comment about how awful a women is who places her baby for adoption. I told her how I felt and she slut-shamed me. Whatever people say, I know I did the best thing for Sarah and now, God works through me to help others. I use foot zoning to help heal other adoptive mothers. I am certified and have been doing it for almost seven years. I hope my story can help someone else believe in themselves and with faith and God's love, everything will work out.

—Rosa Dilworth Reyes

## Twelve
## *Not a Typical Adoption Story*

I am a twenty-four-year-old mother of three, but my baby, my third child I had two months ago, I placed her for adoption. Here's my story.

I experienced postpartum depression when I had my first child, my son. When I had my second child, my daughter Scarlett, the postpartum returned with a vengeance and I was experiencing panic attacks on a daily basis. I was constantly crying and upset, which was not my normal self. I loved my baby Scarlett and never had the thought of hurting her, but I got to the point where I didn't want to live. I went into the hospital to get treatment and it was the lowest point of my life. My marriage was deteriorating. My husband had moved out and since we were separated, he started dating other people. I was discharged from the hospital and felt abandoned and was lonely. If my husband was dating, I felt I should start dating other people too. I met someone and he was providing companionship when we became intimate. A month later, I found out I was pregnant. In the past, I'd struggled with getting pregnant, so this was a huge shock. I didn't tell my husband for a couple of months, but immediately I knew I should place the baby for adoption. I always believed a baby had the right to life. It would have been so easy to arrange for an abortion, but if I really was pro-life, I couldn't let my situation be the exception. That would have been the easy way out, but for me, that wouldn't have been right. Now that I was actually in that position of having an unplanned pregnancy, I really had to put my faith in what I believed.

Everything about my pregnancy pointed me to adoption. This didn't make it easy, but it made it easier. With my other pregnancies, I was so stressed out. I had a lot of medical problems, but with this third pregnancy I was in great health. In a sense, I could let things go because I felt who ever was going to adopt my baby was praying for me. I started looking at the website adoption.com and felt empowered that I was able to choose the family my baby would go to. I was looking for certain things in a family. I wanted them to be married and Christian. I felt it was important that they lived in another state. Looking through family profiles, I saw a picture of a couple and instantly knew they were the parents of my baby. I wanted to give my baby to a family that didn't have children yet. I sent them a message and told them I was nine weeks pregnant. I wasn't sure if it was the right time to contact them, but asked them to send me more information. I was praying all the time that I would remain strong and do the right thing for the baby.

I was still legally married, but my husband had filed for divorce. He'd been dating another girl while we'd been separated and I knew he was having sex with her, but he was so upset at me for becoming pregnant. I could see the hypocrisy in the situation and I knew it wasn't fair for him to judge me when he was having sex, too. I wished he could see I was doing the best I could. For our children's sake, I wanted to work things out, but I wasn't sure if my husband would take me back. He didn't feel like he could forgive me.

With him gone, I wasn't in a position to support our family. The father of the baby I was carrying had told me he wanted to make things work, but he was too young and naïve. I needed to break up with the birth father. It wasn't fair to lead him along when I knew I wanted to better my future. I didn't want him be a part of it, plus I still loved my husband. I knew I wasn't intended to raise this baby and that adoption was the right choice. With everything going on, the baby growing in my belly kept me focused on doing what was best for her.

When I found out I was pregnant, my mom couldn't handle it and moved out of state. She had been living with me and she up and left during my pregnancy so with her and my husband gone, all the bills were my responsibility. I didn't have a car, but my church helped out so much. I wouldn't have gotten by without them. My in-laws weren't in the picture so I was doing this all alone. I was still struggling with postpartum from having Scarlett (she was still a baby), but somehow I was able to handle my postpartum better. My mental health started improving and the postpartum seemed to dissipate. I tried not to think of the baby I was carrying as mine. I didn't want to second guess my decision. Yes, she was still my baby, but she was also meant for another family. At certain points of my pregnancy, I felt excited for my baby's adoptive parents, even happy I could play this important role for them. I was absolutely heartbroken at what was going to happen to me, but at the same time I was so happy for the parents of my baby. They'd wanted a child for such a long time and I was the one who would bring them this gift.

Once I realized I was pregnant, I got my GED and then applied to get into phlebotomy school. This pregnancy propelled me forward in my life. I had to do the best I could with my life for my children. My love for my husband stayed ever present. When I was five months pregnant, I was having trouble taking care of the kids, so even though he was still dating his girlfriend, he moved back in to help out. A couple of weeks later, he broke up with his girlfriend. Was there hope for my marriage after all? It felt like there might be.

In June I went out to meet the couple I'd chosen to adopt my baby. Because I'd already gone through two pregnancies, I wanted to make sure they could experience many aspects of having a baby. I went to the ultrasound with them and although I already knew I was having a girl, I wanted them to experience it firsthand, so I'd kept it a secret. They did a gender reveal. My husband stayed at home with our kids. Although we were still legally married, our relationship was in limbo. I wanted the best thing for this child and didn't want to have her in the middle of all this.

I wanted the adoptive parents to be there for the birth. They came into town and took my kids and I out for ice cream before the baby was born. We'd built a really good relationship and I don't know what I would have done without them. They helped me financially pay for my schooling. They have encouraged me, even shipped me a computer when I needed it. They were placed in my life because I needed somebody. I don't have any family and now I was giving away a daughter, so I needed a family so bad.

I knew I would deliver the baby early, so they drove in a week early because I was having contractions. They took us out to dinner again. I didn't go into labor that weekend, so they drove back to their home state. They came back out that next weekend. When was I going to have this baby? The adoptive parents were taking time off work to come here, so I felt a lot of pressure to go into labor. I needed to have this baby so I could get back to school and they could get back to their lives. It couldn't be put off anymore. My school had already extended my leave by a month. I walked two and one half hours each night and was two centimeters dilated. Sunday morning my water broke, but it still took thirty-six hours of labor to get her out and I was in horrible pain.

After she was born, the nurse asked what I wanted to do. I told her, "I want her mom to have a room and to be in a gown so she can have skin to skin bonding." I wanted her to experience all the beauty of delivering and having a baby. She held our daughter for about an hour. Finally, I had some time with my baby alone. I told her how much I loved her and hoped she wouldn't hate me later. I told her she would have amazing parents and that I wouldn't have picked them any other way. They named her Violet Raeann because my middle name is Ann and the mother's nickname was Ray. The adoptive father prayed for me in the hospital and for Violet. He felt she had chosen to come to earth this way and that she loved me for giving her life. My husband held Violet after she was born and he grew an attachment to her. He loved her and it was difficult for him to say goodbye to her. He loved the adoptive parents too. Because we were married, he had to sign parental rights away and the guy I'd been dating was served papers to sign for adoption.

Now that I'd delivered my baby, my postpartum returned, but not nearly as bad. I still had two young children of my own. Life was so busy and I had a lot of sleepless nights. I had so many stresses on my plate. I couldn't talk to my husband about how I felt and I didn't want to talk to the adoptive parents. There was a piece of my heart that would never be whole again.

When I first went on adoption.com, I'd made a check list of what I wanted in the adoptive parents. I wanted my baby to have a huge family. Now, she has thirty cousins. I wanted her parents to be able to provide for her. Her mom is an artist, which is one of my only true talents. Her dad is really smart and is going to help her with school. Violet will have that perfect balance. Her parents have everything I want for her. I still think of her as my baby and I will be watching, loving and praying for her every day of my life. Some nights I cry all night, but this is what she needs. Some days, I don't know how to be strong, but I find a way. In my worst times, I still know I made the right choice.

I want to visit Violet once or twice a year. Her parents said they would make a trip to see me once a year. They have offered to do Skype. They have helped me in so many aspects and helped me succeed more than I think they can ever truly know. They are incredible people who have helped not only me, but also my family while taking care of the child I gave them. I want them to be recognized for that. I know I've made sacrifices for them, but they've made them for me as well as my family and the kids. I wouldn't be where I am today without them.... absolutely not. They are truly the best two people I've ever met in my life and they continue to be, while still taking care of Violet. They have helped me progress and become the person I always wanted to be. They have been there during the struggles I was dealing with and they will never completely understand what they have meant to me.

I got straight A's from school and am graduating with honors. I'm going to be okay and I'm going to be able to provide for my own children. My husband is still with me and in my heart, I feel we will work things out. We have a deep love and I pray everything we've been through will prevail.

—Anonymous

## Thirteen
## *My Daughter Is My Sunshine*

I had been dating my boyfriend for about four years. I suggested we should break up because he was traveling so much to California for work. A few weeks later, I regretted it and we got back together. My boyfriend and I never had sex, we messed around just enough for me to get pregnant. I think this is a very important part of my story because I didn't think something like that was possible, but it can happen. I'd always kept track of my periods and one day, I realized I was late. I thought, "There is no way," but I took a pregnancy test and to my total and complete shock, I was pregnant. I took a picture of the pregnancy test and sent it over to my boyfriend. I thought we were going to be together, but I found out that in the few weeks we'd broken up, he'd started dating another girl. I confronted him and he said he wanted to be with his new girlfriend, not me. He came with me to doctor's appointments and we went to our church leaders, trying to get back on track. Obviously, I felt judged by some people, but I remained confident. I had my brother call and tell my mom about the pregnancy and when we talked, she told me she understood and she would support me no matter what.

From the very start of my pregnancy, I loved this baby and felt so much love from her to me. I knew I was totally capable of taking care of her. Some people suggested I should place the baby for adoption. I was given a book and all the stories talked about adoption, but I already knew my answer. Still, I prayed about it and although I supported adoption, there was no way I could place my baby. I am a twenty-five-year-old teacher and knew I was able to provide for her. I have a great family support. She was meant to be mine.

The happiest day of my life was when my daughter, Penelope, was born. It was a perfect delivery. She was the cutest little thing and holding her on my chest was the best feeling ever. It was all so amazing. Her dad was there and I had hope we could still be together, but a week after our baby was born, he proposed to his girlfriend. It was tragic, but finally I was able to move on.

I went back to work and as a working mom it was really hard. I loved and adored my baby, so going back to work felt like leaving half of my heart behind. I lived with my parents for a one and a half years and my mom took care of Penelope while I was at work. My parents are so loving and this blessing made leaving my daughter bearable. During this time, I was constantly trying to improve myself. I was following my faith and doing what I knew to be right. I spent all my free time with my daughter. We took walks, played at the park and went to the zoo. She was my absolute favorite person on earth. I would get lost in her adorable personality. Her hair grew in blonde and she would wear piggy tails. She loved everything and just the sound of her voice felt like sunshine. Because of her, I grew into the person I needed to become. I loved the children I taught at my school and did my best at work. I wanted to improve so I could be the mother she deserved. Penelope's dad and I have joint custody and he's a wonderful dad. He is married and Penelope is happy when she spends time with her dad. They are a good family.

When Penelope was ten months old, a man named Josh came back into my life. I had dated Josh when I was twenty-three and we'd remained friends. He moved away to college and I hadn't seen him for about a year, but his sister was hired as an aide in my classroom. She suggested Josh and I go on a date again. Eight months later, he and I were married.

Six months later, we decided to try to have a baby. I became pregnant that week! Although it was a difficult pregnancy, having my second daughter has helped me feel complete and whole. Having babies is not easy, but the love and purpose of holding and nurturing my daughters is my passion. I love being a mom. Josh is a wonderful father and husband. Because of him, I'm able to stay home full-time with my daughters.

—Sarah Moore Jestes

## Fourteen
## *A Pregnancy Scare That Changed My Life*

On a dark winter night in 2014 I was sitting in a car with my mom. We had returned from an outing together and I was anxious to get back home to my then five little children. But something wasn't right. I needed to talk, I needed support. I was struggling to find myself, to find my voice, so in that parked car my mom and I talked for a while. Suddenly, I shared an experience I'd had almost twenty years earlier. It was an experience so dark, so hurtful, I hadn't spoken of it since.

While in college, I started dating a man almost ten years older than me. At first, our courtship was magical, full of first kisses and whispers of a future life together. But soon, I noticed signs he might not be the man I thought he was. He had a temper and became critical. He thought I was stupid because I was vegetarian and pointed it out when we ate together. Not only did he disagree with my goals of getting a college degree, but he mocked my free spirit and creative ideas. He didn't like that I wanted to exercise and made me feel guilty when I went running. No matter what I did, I couldn't be good enough for him. My personality quickly became co-dependent and his problems became mine—in other words, I wanted to fix him. Economically, socially, and emotionally he struggled and his burdens became mine. Before long, I was caught in a web of hurt and an uncertain future. Still, in my heart this was love and I was committed to our relationship. One evening we were at his parents' home and I had homework to finish for finals week. After dinner, I went upstairs to one of the spare bedrooms and started reading on the bed. An hour or so later my boyfriend came upstairs and shut the door. We talked for a few minutes, then he stood up and turned off the light. He came back to me and offered a kiss. Of course I wanted to kiss him; of course I wanted to be close to him. In my desire to please him, to be loved by him, I offered my affection back. Only when he became dominant did I notice how dark and quiet it was all alone in the upstairs bedroom. I didn't want his parents to hear us. I pushed him away, but he pushed back and any trust I had for him dissolved like a forest fire smothered by a midnight rain storm. I found the strength to say "No," but it was like I was talking to a blank page. I was trapped by a man I wanted to love. I was a fool. When he finally did stop and his grip on me weakened, I pushed him off and raced to the bathroom.

I was in shock. Why had he done that? Why had he acted in such a way?

He knew I was saving myself for marriage.

What had just happened? What had I allowed him to do to me?

Reality hit me like the first time I'd witnessed a car accident. I couldn't imagine the worst case scenario. I had to process the car hitting the motorcycle, watching the driver of the motorcycle fly through the air like he was a circus performer shot out of a cannon, not realizing the trauma that can happen in a split second, the minute you hit the ground like a bag of bricks.

A moment ago I was fine. Now, I was broken and scarred for life.

I was a sinner. I was awful. This was the worst thing I could ever imagine.

As I grabbed my things and raced to my car, it dawned on me like a shower of broken glass shards piercing my skin— I could become pregnant.

What if I was pregnant!

On the drive home, I stopped at a drug store and rushed to the aisle of pregnancy tests. I purchased several with the little money I had, ashamed as the cashier rang up my purchases. I wanted to tell him this was not what he might think it was, that I was not that kind of girl, but my body was numb. I couldn't speak. I couldn't cry. Once I returned home, I read the instructions on the back of the box. I had to wait days after my next period should come before the test could determine if I was pregnant or not.

I didn't care. I ripped open the box and right then and there peed on the stick. I waited. The test said I was not pregnant, but I knew I couldn't trust the results. I hadn't followed the directions. I didn't even know when my next period should be. How could I possibly wait? How could I live even another minute without knowing? My life became a living hell.

Several days later, I couldn't get out of bed. It was a gloomy rainy day and I was smothered with heartache. How had I been so stupid! What had I done? Why didn't my boyfriend stop when I'd insisted? He knew I was a virgin. That was certainly not how I would've wanted my first time to be. I had nowhere to turn. My shame was a deep, dark grave covered with layer upon layer of mud. In my desperation, I picked up the phone and called my dad. I asked if he could come to my apartment. I only lived one town away from my parents, so within the hour I heard a knock on my door. I stopped my panicked crying and wiped my eyes. I looked in the mirror and couldn't believe who I'd become in just a few short days. Deranged, insecure and unstable–I no longer recognized myself. When I opened the door ready to fall into my dad's arms, I saw my mom standing right next to him.

My mom was the kindest woman I knew. As a child she prayed with me every night. My mom was my number one fan. She believed in everything I did and was the last person in the world I wanted to see. There was absolutely no way she could know what was going on. It would shatter her perception of me. She couldn't know I was living a lie and that everything she'd taught me my entire life had been thrown away. She couldn't know I might be pregnant, so I did something I'd never done before; I pushed her away.

Even though I felt completely out of control, I took the only control I felt I had. I told my mom I couldn't talk to her, only my dad. She understood and sat on the couch of my living room as my dad and I went out into the cold rainy air. The minute he shut the door to my apartment, I started uncontrollably weeping. He took my hand and rushed me to his car.

"Laura, what is it?" he asked. "What is wrong?"

Not holding back, I told him what had happened. I told him I could be pregnant. I told him I was scared. In a moment of fatherhood glory, my dad did exactly what I needed—he listened. It was some of the most beautiful listening a parent has ever done. There was no judgment, no wasted words, no insincere clichés, just listening. There was plenty of holding, too. My dad held me up when without him, I would have dropped. We drove by my boyfriend's house and it was the first time I'd ever sensed a criminal streak in my dad. I wondered if he was going to go to the door and beat my boyfriend up! Secretly, it would've been fine with me, but I didn't want to say so.

The next few weeks became a struggle of reality vs. living nightmare. The idea I might be pregnant became a permanent stream of poisoned thinking in the back of my mind. I didn't return any my boyfriend's calls. I resolved to never see him again. Suddenly abortion was something to consider. An abortion could save me from the humiliation I might soon be facing. No one would ever have to know, but no – I could never have an abortion! Or could I? Could I convince myself abortion was OK? Perhaps on the surface, but in the dark shadows of my mind, I knew I could never do it. If I was pregnant, I was going to move out-of-state, live with my grandma in Tennessee and give the baby up for adoption. But I was in my last year of college. Would I give up my full-ride scholarship? What about my job? I loved working as a nanny. I would have to give that up, too. So, I carried on with this despicable dance of ideas: tempted by the convenience of abortion only to weep into my pillow with tears of shame for even considering such an idea.

I had school books and a pair of running shoes at my boyfriend's house. I gathered my courage as I had once gathered pinecones as a young girl. I knew the small pinecone could someday become a huge tree, so with a tiny amount of courage that could someday become mighty, I knocked on his door and told him I was there to collect my things. He asked why I hadn't returned his calls. I told him I might be pregnant. He said, "If you are, we could get married." I turned pale and my breathing became sporadic. With a shaking voice and all the strength I could muster, I said, "I could never marry you." Just like that, I never wanted to "fix" him again.

One day, when my reality became too much, I called a childhood friend who'd had a baby out of wedlock several years earlier. I asked how she'd done it and how she felt when first finding out she was pregnant. My friend had much more emotional control over her situation, but her reassurance could not be shared. She tried to convince me everything would work out, but I didn't believe her for a second. Considering her strength, I wondered why I hadn't reached out to her when she'd had her baby. Why had I judged her when she'd been so brave?

I started to imagine what the baby would look like. Could I love this baby under these circumstances? What if the baby looked like my boyfriend? Could I be a good mother? Could I keep the baby? No, because it would force me to stay in contact with my now ex-boyfriend. I never wanted to see his face again, especially in the eyes of my own baby. Abortion could take care of this problem immediately. I could move on quickly and no one would have to know. Maybe I wasn't pregnant and this was all just a nightmare I needed to wake up from. I hoped to have the determination to give the baby up for adoption, yet in my heart I didn't know what I'd do.

One night during this time, I had a dream. I was happy and content, lying on a navy blue couch watching a man play with a baby, our baby. I felt enormous love for both. Although I didn't recognize the man's face, I knew he was my husband and the baby was ours. In the dream, it was Christmas time and I could see a fire burning in the fire place. I ran my hand along a pattern in the fabric of the couch, little tufted pink and cream hearts, but the dream was short-lived. When I woke up, I was back in my nightmare. There was no way my life would ever be ideal and carefree again.

Finally, the day came when I started my period. The relief that washed over me was short lived. I might not be pregnant, but I was still "that girl." What could've been didn't happen, but it could have. Like jumping over a cliff, only to be saved by a passing parachute, I had played Russian roulette with my life and would never be the same. I would never know how I would have handled an unplanned pregnancy.

So, there I was almost twenty years later, telling my mom about one of the biggest heartaches of my life. Why was I telling her now? I wasn't sure, but it felt right. I told her how my secret still affected me and my self-esteem. I told her I never told my husband, that I was too ashamed, and my mom took me in her arms. She held me for a moment and then looked into my eyes.

"Laura, you know you were raped, don't you?"

Wait, what?

I looked back at her, confused by such an idea.

The thought had never crossed my mind.

"You were raped," she said again with more energy. I didn't move. She didn't budge. Her eyes reassured me, but I wasn't having it.

"No, I knew him. He was my boyfriend."

"It doesn't matter, he took advantage of you."

Maybe my mom didn't understand. I was there. I had kissed him. I was his girlfriend. My mom was only trying to take away this burden I'd been carrying. Maybe she thought this was what I wanted to hear. I half-heartedly took her interpretation, but felt she was only trying to console me.

That night I told my husband there was something I needed to talk about. We put our children to bed and sat down in our room to talk. Once again, I picked up my courage as a child picks up pinecones, and I found strength in what my courage could become. What I'd resolved to never tell anyone I was now telling the most important person in my life. I lifted my shame like I had lifted my veil on our wedding day and the love from my husband shone onto my face. I told him about my ex-boyfriend and I felt a little stronger. I told him about the pregnancy test and drew strength from my husband's loving face. I told him I'd considered abortion and felt my husband's compassion. I apologized for keeping secrets and my husband held me in his arms. A moment later, he pulled back and looked into my eyes.

"Honey, you know you were raped, don't you?"

Again, I didn't understand. Didn't my husband know I was responsible for what had happened to me?

Because of the trust and affection I had for my husband, this beautiful man who has always treated me with so much love and respect, I allowed him to teach me. I allowed him to take his perspective and open my heart to the possibility.

I still can't say it. I still can't join the collective group of rape victims and say, "I am one of you." I can't let go of the responsibility I may have had in what happened. I would rather acknowledge other rapes than the possibility of mine. Why was I reluctant to call it rape? I'm still not sure. Was it because I couldn't handle confrontation? If I saw my ex-boyfriend would he call me a liar? I didn't want to justify anything to anyone, especially him. Whatever the label, it still happened and I didn't want to make excuses for my inability to set a boundary. Calling it rape forced me to go back and prove something I didn't want to uncover. In many ways it wasn't about me, it had been about the life we could have potentially made and for some reason God spared me the enormous task of that consequence.

And what about abortion? I was there. I understood the draw, the pull into a procedure that appeared to take away all the pain and uncertainty, the fix and the end of an unwanted chapter. When I thought I might be pregnant, I didn't want to think about the baby growing inside me as a real person, I only wanted to think about my needs. For those few weeks, before I knew if I was pregnant or not, I assumed I *was*. My reality was disappointed parents, dysfunctional relationships and thrown-away dreams, that was the world I lived in. I knew better. I'd been taught a life was a life, but when it was my turn to put another life ahead of mine I didn't know if I could do it. Could I convince myself my situation was the exception? Maybe others shouldn't have an abortion, but was my case different? A born baby was a real baby, unlike the baby I might be carrying. I didn't want to feel any attachment to a baby. I was making the decision with one eye closed and the other eye filled with tears. It was a distortion. A baby was there, but it was not really there. A heartbeat was there, but it started beating without my approval. A human life might be growing without my consent and if I turned away, maybe I wouldn't see it. With what I faced those two weeks, I was nobody's judge.

So much of my life has been shaped by this experience. The worst part has been the low self-esteem, shame and insecurity I've struggled with, but I think it's also made me more sensitive to others who have been abused. I cringe when I read one in three girls will be sexually abused in her lifetime and these are just the reported cases. I'm sure many girls have trusted their boyfriends only to be taken advantage by him.

What is going on with our men? Who is teaching them? Who is setting the example? Why are our men hurting women? With the teaching of sex education needs to come the teaching of self-control, respect for women and sexual consent. This is a most important topic and one that needs a major shift in our communities and nation.

I understand not all unwanted pregnancies come from abusive relationships. Many unplanned pregnancies come from healthy relationships. Many times the father wants to be there and wants to be supportive. Still, I have a goal to reach out to those girls who have or are living in abusive situations and help them. The best way I know to do this is to share my story and hope they will see some part of themselves in what I've experienced and realize they deserve better.

—Laura Lofgreen

## Fifteen
## *I Wish I Could Have Fixed Myself Earlier*

Writing this story is so hard.

My parents were going through a very difficult divorce when I found out I was pregnant. I was 15 years old and got pregnant the first time I had sex. I paid such a price for my son. Here is my story.

When I found out I was pregnant, I knew I couldn't keep the baby. I would place him for adoption. My life was so messed up and I was not going to subject him to that. I would go to bed at night, knowing I couldn't keep him, but so grateful I had him while he was growing inside of me. For a small season, he was mine. I scheduled an appointment at a social service center sponsored by my church. Ironically, before I found out I was pregnant, my mom had come to me and told me she'd had a teenage pregnancy and had placed her baby up for adoption. I had started processing that information when I found out I was also a teenage pregnancy statistic.

During my pregnancy, I developed preeclampsia and was really sick. I had been sick for a couple of months and I didn't know what was going on, so by the time my doctor realized how sick I was it was pretty serious. I was induced seven or eight weeks early. All the odds were stacked against both the baby and me. My kidneys and liver stopped working. I was so unstable, they couldn't transfer me to another hospital. Because my blood wouldn't clot, they couldn't give me a C-section. They did a test before I had my baby and they said he couldn't suck or breathe on his own, but when he was born he weighed five pounds and was twenty inches long. He was perfectly healthy and didn't have to stay in the NICU. My family was with me in the hospital and my dad bawled when he met my baby boy.

At the hospital, while I was recovering, a social worker brought me a stack of papers of families looking to adopt. My mom tried to convince me to keep the baby, but I knew all along he was for someone else. My mom didn't want to see me go through this, but it was what I had to do. I held a certain file in my hand and I just knew this was my baby's family. Spiritually, I knew it was right. I'd never felt anything like it. I truly believed this baby came through me so I could give him to his family. I knew I was doing the right thing, but it was terribly painful. I hated that I couldn't keep my baby, but this was what I needed to do.

There is nothing easy about leaving the hospital without your baby. When I returned to high school, I was lactating. Nobody understood what I was going through and I was stuck somewhere in between adolescence and motherhood. I felt broken. I was suffering on such a level because what I'd been through was a very adult experience. My entire body ached for my baby for a year. I wasn't prepared at all for the consequences of what I was going through. From that moment forward, I spent much of my life desperately missing my son, knowing very well he was not meant to be mine. It was a game of trying to move on, but with a broken heart.

After I'd placed my son, there were no rules in my life. I wasn't a kid anymore. I couldn't have gone back. My parents let me come and go as I pleased. I wish I would have had boundaries and rules and I needed parental guidance. I wanted to cling to my faith, but everything had changed. At church I was treated differently, judged, projected that I would be a bad influence on others and so on. My best friends weren't judgmental. They were so there for me, but I pushed them away. Was I even worthy of love? I had a lot of people who cared about me and they did the best they could to help me, but I had to learn to believe in myself again. I couldn't let them in. I became addicted to pills and was in a dark place.

Somehow, I made it through and when I was twenty, I became pregnant with twins. Although the pregnancy with the twins was unplanned, I was very excited about it. Early on, I had been on bed rest and my body was threatening to go into labor. I knew there was something wrong, but I didn't know the babies weren't going to make it. At five months, the pregnancy took a turn for the worse. My water broke early and I delivered them before I ever met with the specialist. They were born prematurely at twenty-one weeks. When they were born, I was able to greet and hold them. Even though they'd gone to heaven, they were mine. I wanted these little girls so much, my heart would burst. They were absolutely beautiful and the heartache of what I'd already been through intensified. What I later learned was that my twins shared the same blood supply, so they couldn't live outside of me. Medicine has advanced so much, they can probably save babies like mine, but back then this condition was fatal. Looking back at the situation, I'm so glad I didn't know this information while I was pregnant. It would have killed me to know they were sick while I was carrying them. After the twins died, I thought I was being punished by God for my choices.

Finally, when my son turned eighteen years old I reached out to him. His birthday is in March and by June all of our families had met. To hear his family's story, they had so many miracles of how he came into their life. It's incredible now. I am in my son's life and in his parents' life. The peace continues to be reconfirmed to me. Every time I see him, I feel it. I've always had this feeling we'd be best of friends and it's such an honor to be his mother. I'd hoped one day we could hang out and text and that has happened. We have a great relationship. Everything opposite of my life he has and it's amazing. His parents are very successful. His mom was a stay-at-home mom. He has three other siblings, all adopted. Still, he's so much like me. Genetically, it's amazing. He's six foot tall and so handsome. Everything has come full circle.

Meeting my son helped build my self-esteem. When I met him, all the pain I'd experienced in between was worth it. After I met him, I started running every day and lost seventy pounds. I'm happily married now and I love my job. I do international export and facilitate getting vegetable seeds into foreign countries. There are a lot of farms where I live and I work for a seed production company and I am exposed to a lot of cultures that normally I wouldn't get to know about. My husband is perfect for me. He is very structured and committed. I'm all over the place and he keeps me rooted. He was settled before I came along and he gave me a sort of platform to grow from. He was so secure and didn't have issues, so he helped me become healthier. My story isn't sugar-coated and things didn't happen overnight, but little by little I kept improving. I still have a ways to go, but sharing my story has been another step towards healing.

I wish I would have worked on myself earlier. For fifteen years, I've struggled. It wasn't until I had my daughter in 2009 that I finally started healing in big leaps and bounds. My self-esteem was horrible. My friends who'd tried to get back into my life that I'd pushed away, I was ready to try again.

My daughter gave me the reason to fix myself. When she was two, I had to have a hysterectomy. Although there's a thirteen-year gap, my son and my daughter have this incredible relationship. Seeing them together makes it all worth it. My daughter just worships him.

I would say to anyone going through an unplanned pregnancy, whatever you decide, please go to counseling. I needed help and didn't realize it. I wish I would have fixed myself earlier. I wish I would have talked and opened up. I needed help. Please seek help so you don't lose yourself. You will never be the same and I didn't understand that.

—Anonymous

## Sixteen
## *Loving My Baby is My Perfect Expression*

I found out I was pregnant on my 42nd birthday. I was happily married, but the pregnancy was unplanned and I was devastated. I didn't want to be pregnant. I was too old and felt overwhelmed. I was discouraged and didn't see how it would all work out. My husband was sympathetic to how I felt, but he was thrilled to have another child. I'm so thankful I had his support and encouragement. We both loved being parents to our five children and he felt like a sixth child was a blessing, but I didn't know how I was going to do it.

My baby came at a difficult time in my life. I had four sons ranging in age fifteen to age seven, and my fifth child, my little daughter, would be starting kindergarten soon. Finally, I could move on with either my career in writing or working my other business of furniture restoration. I was overweight and had horrible varicose veins. There were other personal reasons I didn't feel I could handle this and a baby was not in the plans. With my pregnancy I had debilitating morning sickness, doubt, uncertainty, emotional turmoil, physical exhaustion, but I also had faith. Faith was what I held on to when my world felt out of control and in return for my small nine-month sacrifice I received a baby, a baby that changed my world for the better.

The feelings I'd had while pregnant—the verdict I couldn't handle another baby, that it would be too much, that I would never survive—that verdict had been overturned. My baby did not result in lost opportunities, but freedom, liberation and love at a level I'd never understood. In other words, my sacrifice of having my baby had significant purpose. It *was* the purpose. Delivering a child brought me to a plateau I wouldn't have reached without him. I named my son Canyon and he was and is the key to the growth I've experienced. Having my baby in my arms, rocking him to sleep, playing, giggling, comforting him when he's crying—all these experiences literally change me physically. I can feel it. A part of me grows and stretches yet also feels secure, validated and incredibly loved. There is this desire to express myself through loving and taking care of him. Mothering him is my expression. His perfect head has received too many kisses to count. His little body, the way he wraps it around my hips when I jolt out the door, how he fits so perfectly into my arms like a jockey riding a rickety horse, I just love every minute of it.

Now that he is eighteen months old, he has started kissing me and those kisses are full of drool. He loves me without words, only through actions. He kisses me with eyes wide open, his little pouty breath warming my cheeks and we lock lips. This little baby makes me be present, grateful and focused on giant moments of split-second heart-warming experiences.

He's a baby. My baby. I paid such a price for him. At first, I didn't think I could take on such a task of another baby, and here's what I have to say to anyone considering an abortion – PLEASE

HANG ON. I promise, with all the complications and personal obstacles, with all the work and uncertainty, to get one of those kisses from my baby I paid such a high price for, it is worth it. Even as he sleeps, I watch and wait, ready for more of everything he has to offer. From his baby babble to the primal way he needs me, if my arms were empty I would be searching my *entire life* to fill them with something meaningful. A baby is impossible to replace.

Don't let the world tell you anything is more important than your baby. I've had more help with this baby than any of my other children. People step up. My husband and my kids are the number one reason this baby is so happy and well-adjusted. They are constantly reaching out to him. Each has their own special game, songs and experiences. I could never provide the education, life lessons, and personal development to my older kids the way this baby does. He's our family's peacemaker. We all strive to be better and do more because of him.

This is what I've learned since having my unplanned pregnancy:

**1.** God will perform mighty miracles in your life when you do difficult things. Having Canyon has allowed me to see what God can do for me with my unique personality and life experiences. When I thought I was weak, He gave me strength. What I thought I would just "get through best I could" has turned into one of the most tender and beautiful experiences of my life. I have more love in my heart than I thought possible. My faith has increased tremendously.

**2.** The innocence and vulnerability of a baby has absolutely come alive for me. I have such a sense of worth and love for him while fulfilling his needs. When Canyon was born, he was placed on my chest crying. I soothed his little back and spoke to my son, "Momma's here, Momma's here." He immediately stopped crying. Later when he cried, I again spoke to him. I couldn't believe how responsive he was to my voice. Just speaking to him in a soft tone soothed him.

**3.** A baby can offer healing. I have had the privilege and comfort of holding my newborn baby while working through my emotions I'd had while pregnant. Had I really not wanted him? Did I think he would be a burden? I became horrified about abortion. More wars for life are fought in a mother's womb than anywhere else in the world. Some nights I will get him out of his crib and hold him because of the love and energy I feel from his little soul. I tremble to think only months earlier he was the size of the babies who have been killed by abortion.

**4.** Although I've never had an abortion, I'd considered one when I'd had a pregnancy scare at the age of twenty-five. I have a respect for babies I've never had before. There have been fifty-nine million abortions in America since Roe vs. Wade. In the African American community, more babies are aborted every year than born. I look at my son Canyon as a survivor. He will bless me throughout my life. Every baby is special. I think there is light shining from new babies and their experience on earth should be loved and celebrated.

**5.** A baby can change the tone of a home. There is more patience, love and joy. My kids take turns because they are all so excited to hold the baby. I feel the lessons learned about the dignity of life and purity of a baby will forever impact my children. In other words, my son is not just my son, but somebody else's brother, cousin, grandson and friend.

It is my commitment to never forget what I've learned from Canyon.

I know people do extraordinary things with their lives. They travel, study and more. Some say having a baby means you can't fulfill your dreams. I disagree. My baby is my Mt. Everest, with all the training, dreams, setbacks, visions, occasional oxygen mask and life-changing accomplishment that comes with it. At the peak, he is my beautiful view of the world, my breathtaking scenery and the wind blowing through my hair. He is my PhD, my higher education and confirmed thesis.

The world tries to convince women they can only do one or the other. Since I've had this baby, I've written a memoir, taken charge of my health, gone cliff jumping, signed up for improv classes and more. I did not have to choose between my baby and other experiences life has to offer. I can do both.

I want every woman to know their baby is just as special, that if they give their baby a chance they will know what I know . . . that a baby is more valuable, more life-changing and more important than anything else in life.

When everything else fell away and I could see through the eyes of love, I knew my baby was worth it. His presence alone is enough, but the physical warmth of his body next to mine makes every cell of my body sing. In finding him, I lost myself and away went all the rationality that having a baby would be too difficult. I'm stronger than I knew and my complaining only made me weak. When in frustration I voiced out I wasn't strong enough to care for another baby, something said back to me, "Be stronger," and I knew it was the voice of God. I had that choice, to be stronger than the negativity, the societal pressure and uncertainty. I want my son to know I stand for him and I want women to know people like my son deserve a chance, that we don't want to just wipe out such charisma and beauty before they even have a chance. How many babies just like Canyon are aborted before their mothers get to know how amazing they are?

Having a baby is hard and messy. He's one year-old now and still, some days I wonder how I'm going to do it, but I have this motivation deep in my heart that will never burn out. It tells me my baby is worth it, that I will never regret raising my baby and that in his smile, in his laughter, I've found my greatest joy.

A baby is worth it. A living, breathing, one-of-a-kind baby is more dynamic and diverse than any experience the world has to offer. My baby makes me better. My baby is my beautiful teacher. My baby smiles and I have seen heaven. When we dance, when we cuddle, when he toddles towards me with an open picture book I feel a love that expands the cells in my body. Breathing reminds me I'm having a physical experience, but the love I feel insists the experience is much, much bigger.

—Laura Lofgreen

## Seventeen
## *Because Of My Unplanned Pregnancies, My Life Was Redeemed*

"Do another one," I said to the nurse as she told me that my pregnancy test was turning positive. After the third positive test, I had no choice but to accept the results as truth. Just two weeks earlier I had been in the emergency room with severe abdominal pain and vomiting but they had given me a blood and urine test to rule out pregnancy and sure enough, they were both negative. They scheduled a follow up appointment with a local gynecologist for two weeks later but in the meantime, I did not participate in any sexual activity with my boyfriend. I had only been with my boyfriend for two months so I was paranoid of the thought that he had given me a sexually transmitted infection, not to mention that I was quite literally buckled over in pain from whatever had been going on inside of my body. Now I knew. I was pregnant and after a quick trip to the radiologist it was confirmed by the evidence on the screen that my baby had been caught up in my fallopian tube and had miraculously moved into my uterus, this is what had caused all the pain.

The first words out of my boyfriend's mouth were, "You know you're having an abortion, right?" Of course, I was, that is just what you do when you find out you're pregnant and you don't want to be. On the long drive back to his house my mind just swirled with stress and anxiety as I faintly heard his nonstop words drill into my head about how unfair it would be to 'stick him with a kid' and how his own father was still having child support payments garnished from his paycheck. It was all about him and how inconvenient my pregnancy was and how it was my fault and that he would not be burdened in any way shape or form. I had to 'take care of this' or else. After I dropped him off my next stop was home. How was I going to face my mom? On the short drive back to my house I formulated a plan. I would walk in, find my mom, spill it all out, and quickly disappear into my room. You see, my mom and I were not exactly close and our mother–daughter relationship was anything but healthy and normal. We were more like dysfunctional friends and party buddies. I tended to be a little more responsible as far as behavior was concerned. I often had to apologize for my mom and beg her to change her mind about certain things to spare her consequences. Yet my mom knew how to pull the mom card. In the blink of an eye she could flip her switch and go from fun and carefree to enforcing harsh punishments and revoking the most basic of privileges and her punishments rarely fit the crime so to speak. I honestly had no idea how my mom was going to handle the news about my pregnancy but I knew that I couldn't get away with keeping something this big from her.

Upon walking in the door to my house I went into the living room and approached my mom. I just looked her square in the eye and said, "I just found out that I'm pregnant but don't worry, I'm going to have an abortion so you can pretend I never told you this because soon it will be as though it never happened!" Then I turned and went to walk into my room according to the plan I had established on my drive home. My mom launched out of her seat on the couch, and for a split-second I was fearful of a physical attack, but she immediately responded that I would NOT be having an abortion. Honestly, I was shocked. My mom did not identify as a pro-life person by any means and I kind of thought that having an abortion would be the responsible thing to do in my situation. She quickly followed her response with adding that what I planned on aborting was HER grandchild. She continued with telling me that she would be right there for me, every step of the way. She would help me with diapers, child care, or anything else but that I just could not abort her grandbaby. Now I was in a difficult position to choose between my mom or my boyfriend. Which of the two was I more afraid of angering by not submitting to their demands? Ultimately, I chose life, but with reluctance. I was more afraid of losing my mom's support than that of my boyfriend that I was already on the verge of breaking up with anyways.

It only took a few weeks into our relationship before he started controlling me and restricting me from hanging out with friends and family. He had also already behaved in ways that made me question whether he would cheat on me. Ultimately, I didn't see him as a long-term committed partner so I didn't value his opinions as highly. At the same time, these same reasons caused me to really want to go through with the abortion behind my mom's back. I did NOT want to be attached to this guy for the rest of my life. What kind of life would that make for the baby, to never know their parents as a couple, to be forced to go back and forth between homes, or to simply be rejected and abandoned by their father. I felt so much pressure on my shoulders to make the 'right choice' but I simply defaulted to what my mom told me. She would be there for me 100%, she would take care of me and the baby and make sure that we always had what we needed. We didn't have the best relationship but I trusted her on this one, after all, she was a mom so she had more experience in this category than both me and my boyfriend.

After I made my final decision to keep the baby I broke the news to my boyfriend. This resulted in a prompt breakup. He told me that he wanted nothing to do with the baby and that I was free to do what I wanted but to leave him out of everything. It was hard the first couple of weeks to face the reality that I was going to be a single mom but eventually he came back around. He even went to my mom and had a heart-to-heart with her and expressed that he wanted to make peace with her and the rest of my family. She told him that it would be best for him to move in with us and incorporate into our family so we could all get to know each other better. At first all was well and everyone got along but soon he started hiding away in my room and avoiding everyone. After just a couple of weeks back together we ended up in an emotionally heated blow-up. He had been drinking all day and he was behaving irrationally. Eventually I went to my room to grab his things to place into his arms, to tell him to leave, and he followed me through the house. We were both yelling and screaming at each other and the argument escalated quickly. As I turned to him with his belongings, he shoved me backwards onto my bed and my mom walked into my room and stopped him before he could physically assault me. He told me that the baby wasn't his and that he hoped we both died as my mom escorted him out the door and sent him packing. The next day my mom took me to the women's safety and resource center to help me obtain a restraining order against him.

It felt like my whole life was falling apart and before I would have just hidden my sorrows behind drugs, alcohol, and promiscuous relationships but now I was pregnant so I was experiencing the full range of emotions without anything to numb me. Everything that I had experienced over the previous months was just a small taste of the terrible things that this season of life really held for me. Shortly after the violent breakup I had with my boyfriend, my mom's fiancé died in a car accident. I was supposed to be the one driving that day but at the last minute he and my mom decided to make a date day of the errand that I was supposed to be running. My mom was such a mess and she was taking out a lot of her grief on me, I also felt extremely guilty since I should have been the one driving that day. Maybe if I had fought harder to be the one to run the errand, the accident wouldn't have happened or it would have been me, not him. As I already mentioned, my mom was not the healthiest example for me. Her fiancé was only a year and a half older than me, he had been one of my best friends from high school. If I had never introduced them then maybe he would have still been alive. I even started feeling guilty for being pregnant. I was so sick each day that I didn't have a lot of energy left over to be there for my mom in her grief. My hormones and emotions were all out of whack as well so I just felt really disconnected from the whole situation, like I was watching everything unfold from the outside looking in yet I was right in the middle of it all. I was numb and raw all at once. I was barely able to come up for air before the next tragedy struck.

The morning of November 19, 2001 became my rock bottom. I was three and a half months into my unplanned pregnancy with a restraining order on my baby's father and was amid grief after the unexpected loss of a close friend, and nothing could have prepared me for what I was about to experience. The phone rang and it was for my mom. After I was unable to find her in her room I had assumed that she had gone for a walk. I took a message and hung up the phone only to see her walking shoes at the door. It occurred to me that maybe she was in her bathroom so I went in to check. The closer I got to her bathroom door, the more uneasy I became. The light was on yet it was bright outside and there was no noise to suggest that she was in the shower or moving around. As I turned the corner my eyes fixated on her bathtub, she was in it, beneath the still water. She was curled up on her left side in the fetal position. I ran through the house screaming that mom was dead then quickly made my way back into the bathroom with the smallest glimmer of hope that just maybe she wasn't. My arms shot into the water, grabbed her shoulders, and pulled her up. Her body stayed in the same position as rigor mortis had already set in. She was cold, stiff, and clearly beyond hope of resuscitation. As I sat on the edge of her tub holding on to her to prevent her slipping back under the water, so many things just kept swirling my mind. She promised to be there for me, she told me that everything would be okay. I chose not to have an abortion because my baby was her grandchild not because I had some deep conviction about the sanctity of life. The horrific images of that day will forever be burned into my memory. I will never forget the sight of her under the still water in her long white dress or the blue bowl of the few leftover pills on the edge of the tub. Life got hard for my mom and she bailed, my life was still hard and the way she chose to leave this world only added insult to injury. I wanted to just give up and check out too.

The night after my mom's suicide I found myself sitting in her closet. I just wanted to feel close to her so I put on one of her dresses and all her jewelry. As I looked down I saw a belt lying on the floor and for some reason I picked it up and tightened it around my neck. It didn't take but a moment for my airway to become restricted and for my eyes to feel as though they were bulging from their sockets. My body became tingly and numb as my mind began racing. Could I live with myself if my baby died because of my suicide? I guess I would never know as I would be dead. Did I want my last conscious thought to be that my baby was going to die because of me? As I felt my breath slow to desperate gasps I cried out in my mind, "If there is really a God out there then take me to be with my mom or get me out of this house and change my life because I just can't do this anymore!" In that very moment, I heard someone at a distance calling my name, "Where's Meagan? Where's Meagan?" In a split-second decision, I decided to get the belt off my neck, I had been through the mental health system as a teen and I didn't want to go back into mandatory counseling or be held on a suicide watch. I still wanted to die, but I didn't want to be interrupted, I even remember thinking that I would just wait until the baby was born and try again. As I managed to get the belt off my neck the closet door opened. It was a friend that I had met the previous spring. He had been at the grocery store in our small town and heard what happened to my mom so he got in the car and drove straight to my house. He came to the door and asked for me, prompting everyone to walk through the house asking where I was. Just as I managed to get the belt off my neck and take in a huge gasp of air, the closet door opened and it was my friend. He came into the closet, bent down, picked me up, and carried me out to his car. I don't know if he was able to quickly assess what he had interrupted, but to this day, I still don't know why he literally showed up at my house to remove me, I do however recognize this event as an immediate answer to my desperate plea to God.

Although my life was a complete disaster, the world didn't stop spinning. I was pregnant and had to keep up with my doctor's appointments and begin planning for how to care for my baby. I secured a job and I managed to get through each day by sheer necessity. The time came to give birth and I welcomed my sweet little girl in May of 2002. She looked just like my mom so that was hard for me but looking into her sweet little face made me feel like my life really could be worth living after all. In fact, being a new mom flooded me with all kinds of hormones and emotions and I began to reevaluate many of the decisions I had made in recent years and months. Staring at my daughter made me think of her father. Had I been too harsh in obtaining a restraining order? Did I only do it because my mom made me? Would my daughter grow up to resent me because I "kept her father away"? Even though there was a restraining order in place I decided to reach out to him and give him the opportunity to meet and bond with his daughter. At first I would let him sit in the other room with my daughter for an hour, and then he would leave. Then I allowed him to stay longer and longer over the course of a few weeks. Eventually I allowed him to sleep in the spare room and give the opportunity to care for our daughter in the middle of the night, he would just knock on my door when she needed to nurse and then I would lay her back down next to him when I was done. When she was about three weeks old I finished nursing her and tiptoed into the spare room to give her back to her father, he woke up and helped me situate her. We sparked a brief conversation and one thing led to the next as we reflected upon this precious little life that we had created together. By the time the sun came up we had made the decision to start fresh with a clean slate and get back together as a couple. He moved back into the house within days and we just made it a point to never be seen in public together until the restraining order expired about six months later. I don't know if I was blinded by the hormones and sleep deprivation or if I was just desperate to have some type of support in my life considering the absence of my mom.

It didn't take long for the abuse to start up again, even before the restraining order was up. With one simple phone call I could have had the order enforced but I was afraid that I would get in trouble too and have my daughter taken away. I also felt guilty. I had been with two other people while I was pregnant with my daughter and when we got back together he asked me if I had been with anyone else and I told him the truth. Daily I was reminded that I had been with other people while HIS child was inside of my body. The abuse was never physical but on any given day I was screamed at, called derogatory names, deprived of needed supplies to care for my daughter while also not being allowed to work outside the home. I was also not allowed to talk on the phone to any friends or family. My daily routine revolved around keeping him happy, even if it meant choosing to meet his demands before I met a basic need for my daughter such as changing her diaper or giving her a bottle. He was also sexually abusive toward me. I was not allowed to tell him no and he made very degrading demands of me. I truly felt helpless. At one point, I wanted to start going to church but he denied my request. He just spent his days consuming excessive amounts of alcohol and his evenings treating me like his property. My home life was very controlled and I just did what I was told to keep the peace. At one point though, a friend of mine had lost her dad to suicide and she contacted me to see if I would go to church with her for her first night back after everything had happened. She wanted to be accompanied by someone who understood what it was like to lose a parent in this manner. Surprisingly, he said yes, it came at a price though. Our new routine consisted of me and my daughter going to church on Wednesdays and dropping him off at his drinking buddy's house. Those nights were always the worst but after being at church I felt like I had a little more strength to endure his verbal assaults. One night at church the message was about rejecting things that kept us away from God. I felt like my eyes were opened that night and I went home and broke up with my boyfriend. Not only was he keeping me from a relationship with Christ, but I also sat back and realized that I would never want my daughter to be with a man like him. If he wasn't good enough for my daughter then why should I settle for the abuse for one more day, I was done!

My daughter was thirteen months old when her dad and I broke up for the final time but I had basically been a single mom her entire life. Her dad rarely even changed a diaper after the first couple of months. Without him around to control me, I became much more independent and within days of our breakup I secured a job and child care. Now, I wasn't aware of how damaged I was from the years of abuse coupled with the traumatic events I had endured. My self-worth was nonexistent and I believed the words that my ex had drilled into my head, such as 'no one will ever want to be with you, you're nothing but used up trash with a kid.' From the time I lost my virginity at thirteen years old, I had engaged in promiscuous behavior, and it would take me years of healing to connect this behavior to the sexual abuse and neglect that I experienced in my childhood. I quickly fell back into those old ruts. Promiscuity was my security blanket. My new routine included frequenting the bar and flirting with lots of guys. I felt that I really needed to overcompensate for being a single mom so I resorted to dressing provocatively and being quick to engaging in physical relationships with the guys I was meeting. I started drinking a lot more than I ever had as a wild teen and was leaving my daughter at overnight sitters on a regular basis. During one of my wild nights I ended up reconnecting with the guy who rescued me out of my mom's closet the night I attempted suicide. We had engaged in a short-term relationship during my pregnancy but we really didn't have a lot in common so we peacefully parted ways and remained friends, although I wasn't allowed to talk to him when I was still with my ex. Looking back, I think I was excited about reconnecting with him simply because I had endured so many hours of brutalizing verbal attacks over having dated him while I was pregnant with my ex's daughter. Being with him and feeling wanted by him kind of felt like a deserved reward after a yearlong nightmare was inflicted upon me in his name. Because I was already a single mom, I was much more aware of the reality of risking pregnancy so I scheduled an appointment to get on birth control. I had been going to church on a consistent basis and was even plugged into some smaller bible study groups. I remember thinking that I probably shouldn't be engaging in sexual activity outside of marriage but that I wasn't a virgin so all those rules didn't really apply to me. I had heard many talks about purity but I wasn't pure anymore. According to my ex, I was used up trash and that's exactly how I felt so what did it really matter if I was having premarital sex, I mean I already had a baby. I just wanted to be responsible and prevent another unplanned pregnancy.

The day I went into the health department for my appointment the nurse asked if I had engaged in unprotected sexual activity within the last seventy-two hours, and my answer was yes. Without batting an eye or so much as a word of explanation, she placed a pill in her hand and extended it to me with the instructions to take it. For some reason, I hesitated and asked her why. She told me that it would prevent me from becoming pregnant if I were to conceive from the unprotected sex I had just reported to her. I can't explain what it felt like but I had this overwhelming urge to resist taking that pill. I told her that if my body was in the process of conceiving a baby because of that unprotected encounter that I was not going to intervene and play God, furthermore, if I became pregnant, it would not be my child's fault so why should I punish this little person for my own sins! I told her that if I became pregnant that it was my own consequence that I was willing to face but that I was not in a moral position to pick and choose who should be allowed to live or deny the potential for their existence. It was in this moment that I realized for the first time ever that I was pro-life, also that I was a huge hypocrite. Here I was giving a moral lecture to this nurse but I was the fornicating Christian in the room. After carrying a baby to term and experiencing life within my own body, I KNEW exactly what it was that would be denied if I stopped the conception process. Plus, I knew that I wasn't going to end up pregnant again, that's why I was at this appointment to get on birth control pills. If only I had known then what I do now about the dangers of hormonal contraceptives, I would have never walked out of that building with a six-month supply. The instructions I took with me told me to wait until the first Sunday after my next period to start taking the pills so I placed them on my bathroom shelf and went about my day to day routine. I was a busy mom, working up to three jobs at any given time and balancing my work, home, and parenting schedule while still trying to squeeze in time to do my own thing. I began to feel more and more convicted about going to church while living a double life and I started talking to my boyfriend more about going to church with me and telling him that I really wanted to live my life in a pleasing way to God. I knew that his mom went to church with me so I hoped deep down that he would consider joining us. I had also hoped that he would fall in love with me and want to be a father to my little girl as her dad had pretty much ceased all contact at this point, just eight months after our split. I was growing tired of late night drinking and uncommitted sex, I wanted a family, but I wanted it to happen the right way.

I've always been a prankster so as April of 2004 approached, I decided to pull the whole 'I'm pregnant, April fool's!' on my boyfriend as he was planning on staying over at my place on the last day of March. Then I got to thinking about how embarrassing it would be if I pulled that prank and later found out that I was actually pregnant so I decided to take a test. I hadn't started my period since my appointment so my birth control pills still sat on the shelf unopened. Then I started thinking back to how long it had been since I had my last period. I decided to take the test right before we went to bed so that I could tell him first thing in the morning and know with certainty that I wasn't. That's when I saw the test turn positive, while he sat unknowingly on my bed in the other room. This time was much different than the first time I had a positive pregnancy test. The moment I saw that plus sign I saw this perfect little boy with olive skin and green eyes and I was in love, then I freaked out. Even though I was terrified, I was filled with absolute peace. Having already gone through this once and surviving the hellish circumstances that pelted me through my whole pregnancy, I knew that I would be okay. I knew that I had what it took to be a mom. Still, my hands shook as I walked out to my room clutching the test behind my back. I climbed up onto my bed and looked at my boyfriend and told him that I had planned on pulling a prank on him in the morning but that it backfired on me. Then I pulled the positive test out from behind my back and showed it to him. He laughed, I joined in. It wasn't quite the reaction I was expecting but it was certainly better than I expected and what I had experienced the first time I found out I was pregnant. He just kept laughing and then was like, "Oh that was a good one, nice try." He thought I was joking. I stopped laughing and told him with a very serious tone and expression that I wasn't kidding. I then explained it all to him again, that I wanted to make sure I wasn't actually pregnant before I told him I was as a prank, then I got to thinking and realized I was a couple weeks late and that yes, in fact, my test was really positive, I was seriously pregnant. Then he got mad, then he started laughing again. At this point we got ready for bed and he was totally convinced that I was joking. I didn't want to press the issue and I was also in shock and experiencing a confusing wave of emotions myself so we just went to bed and I figured we would work through this another day. After a few weeks of holding to my story he finally believed me, he had to accept that I was pregnant. We told his parents and naturally they were not thrilled as we had been keeping our relationship a secret so it was like a double shocker to them. Not only were we a couple but now we were having a baby. It was a lot to take in all at once. This is when he told me that he needed some space to sort out his feelings. He took a job about an hour and a half away and told me that he would call me the following weekend. We didn't end up having contact again until I was about six months pregnant and even then, we only spoke a handful of times. To add the icing on the cake, he also had a girlfriend with five kids who called him dad but he was demanding that I take a paternity test.

In the meantime, I was once again pregnant out of wedlock and completely alone except for my daughter. Who would ever want to be with me, a single mom with two kids from two dads? It was in these broken moments that I began to really dig deep into my childhood and adolescent years and could identify some breaking points where I chose the wrong fork in the road. It seemed like the bad decisions that others had made for me had set me up to make many of my own bad decisions and they just all compounded in a gigantic mess that was my life. I felt worthless, unlovable, used up, and abandoned. How did I keep ending up with these uncommitted guys who wanted my body at their own convenience but nothing more? It was a cold hard slap in the face but I realized that I was attracting these men because of how I presented myself. The way I was living my life wasn't exactly a big selling point to a wholesome godly man. I was settling for less than God's best for me and the consequences that came with those decisions no longer just affected me, they were affecting my children. How many more children from how many more fathers would I end up having if I stayed on the road I was on? Abortion would never again be an option for me so the only other option for me was to change my behavior and that is just what I did. I made a commitment to abstinence until my wedding night, even though I figured that no one would ever want to be with me. I thought that the only guys who would want someone with my past and present circumstances were the same uncommitted or abusive people that I had already been with and the men that held the values and morals that I wanted in a husband would never settle for someone like me. Still I made my commitment to change and I began separating myself from my old life. It was a long and lonely pregnancy but I kept to a very simple life. I worked, went to church and bible studies, and spent time with my daughter, that was it. Surprisingly, the people at church were very accepting of me in my situation. No one gave me dirty looks or whispered behind my back, at least nothing ever made its way back to me. The most awkward thing that happened was actually pretty funny. I was standing in a small group of women and a gal that I hadn't seen in a while paused from several feet away and exclaimed loudly, "Oh my gosh! I didn't know you got married!" I turned my head around to look for the woman rocking a new ring on her finger but then she got my attention and said, "No you, when did you get married?" With complete bewilderment, I told her that I hadn't gotten married. Then her face turned beet-red and she whispered with embarrassment that she was sorry, she thought I was pregnant. I looked back at her and said, "I am," I didn't know who was more embarrassed between the two of us, but I sure get a good laugh now when looking back. Aside from this random moment, everyone was anxiously awaiting the new arrival to the nursery.

My daughter was only two and I didn't have a lot of experience of what healthy parenting looked like, so I started getting involved in the children's ministry at the church. I thought it would be a good way for me to learn how to work with kids and that I could take what I learned into consideration in how I interacted with my own kids. It didn't take long for me to develop respect and admiration for the children's pastor. He was so fun and silly and he interacted with the kids like you would expect a father to. It was nice to see my daughter bond with a positive male role model. Still, I was a single mom still pregnant with my second kid from a second father so I avoided him like the plague outside of church-related activities so that people didn't think I was trying to 'find a man.' Over time, we began running into each other more and I eventually found out that it was him who left the giant bag of little boys' clothing on my porch. He had been married and had a little boy. His wife left four months into the marriage and said she had never really loved him. He spent two and a half years trying to get her to come back to him before he finally agreed to sign the papers so she could marry the man she moved away with. Our boys were only eight months apart so he saved up a bunch of baby clothes to pass along to me once he found out that I was having a boy. Witnessing his love and devotion for his estranged wife inspired me to pray for a husband like him. I started a prayer journal and poured my heart out to God, I dreamed big and with hope that maybe someone as forgiving and loving as this man would come into my life.

November of 2004 rolled around and I gave birth to my little man on Thanksgiving Day. The moment I had seen my pregnancy test turn positive I caught a glimpse of a little boy with olive skin and green eyes, I was now holding the perfect replica of the little boy I had seen. Life got crazier as I adjusted to being a single mom to two little ones running around but no matter what I had to remove from my schedule I still found a way to make it to church and continue serving in the children's ministry. Over time, I developed feelings for the children's pastor and strongly considered ceasing my volunteering in his classroom but he eventually disclosed his feelings to me as well. I couldn't believe that the man who inspired me to pray for a man like him, turned out to be the man who would fall in love with me. We knew that building a life together would be complicated as a blended family but we went through an extensive amount of premarital counseling and maintained very high boundaries with the kids as not to confuse them. We were married in November of 2006 with three kids in tow, they made for the perfect flower girl and ring bearers. We were just two single parents that had come from completely opposite directions. I always tell people that he did everything the right way and still suffered heartache and loss and I did everything the wrong way yet when I submitted myself to God and His plans, I was still able to partake in the blessings of a Christ-centered marriage and family. We are now both able to share in God's redemptive work. We are now a family of six, having one more child together. My children's fathers have never fully come around but thanks to the beautiful gift of adoption, my daughter now shares a last name with me and her new daddy. My husband has yet to legally adopt my son but we were at least able to make a court-certified plan in the event of my death that allows him to gain full custody so our family won't be separated. After overcoming childhood abuse, a life centered around substance abuse and promiscuity, and surviving two unplanned pregnancies, my mom's suicide, and the difficulties that come with being a single mom, I now know that with God, all things are possible and that He will restore the years that the locusts have eaten. God places the lonely and the broken into families and He will not abandon the needs of the fatherless and the widow. God will not bring a child into existence without already having a plan for their future. My children have the most amazing father and even though their lives didn't start out ideally, they would both share how grateful they are to be alive. My first unplanned pregnancy quite literally saved my life and my second inspired changes in my life that have since healed me and made me whole in Christ.

—Meagen Weber

# Eighteen

## *Open Adoption Gave Us a Better Chance at Life*

One late night at a sleepover just weeks after my sixteenth birthday, I saw those two pink lines on a pregnancy test.

When I told the father of my baby about my pregnancy, he did not say very much except that he was not ready to parent and suggested adoption. I dismissed the idea because I was set on parenting with or without him. We tried to stay together for a little longer and I had hoped a baby would keep us together, but it didn't. We had grown apart.

Having to deal with a breakup while pregnant sent me into a depression. My situation became the lowest time in my life as I felt covered in shame and guilt. I missed days of school, not because I felt physically bad, but because I could not stop crying. There were mornings I would catch my own eyes in the mirror and not recognize myself and what I had become. I knew this wasn't who I was supposed to be and how my life should turn out.

I told my family about my pregnancy and was met with support and love overall, though we still had many emotions and plans to process together. Abortion was mentioned but a deep sense of morality was in me. I knew this baby was here for a reason and deserved a chance at life. The first thing my stepmother told me was, "Thank you for choosing life. You could have made a different choice in secret—but you chose life." Her response was a spark of hope.

My mother took me to counseling once she found out to help us navigate the stormy waters our life felt then. Adoption was brought up again by my social worker, but I still dismissed the idea because I wanted to parent. I wanted something to love and to love me back. That is why I had gotten pregnant in the first place—I was trying to fill a void in my heart with love. I was ready to sacrifice everything: prom, dating, getting a job, going off to college, you name it. I was ready to take it on because I desperately wanted her with me. I wanted to be her mother.

While I wanted so desperately to do whatever I could to sacrifice aspects of my teenage childhood for her to be with me, it never gave me peace. I struggled with my decision to parent or place. I spoke with other teen moms, and birth moms online to help gain insight. I continued to be stubborn in what I wanted and not what I knew was best. There was a war going on inside of me, between logic and love. How logical was it for me to be a mother at only sixteen, with no job, not even a license to drive, a junior in high school, and no father for her? However, I loved her so much already and I couldn't bear the thought of any choice other than her being with me.

One spring day when I was seven months pregnant, God lifted a veil from my eyes on a mountain top while I was hiking with my mom. My view of loving my daughter finally became not of *me* and what I wanted. It was a softened heart to give her a chance at her best life. While tears fell, cleansing me of my weighted decision and the shame of my past choices, it was in that moment that I chose to surrender to God and His plan of adoption. It was in that moment that I finally had peace and the war within me stopped. I realized that love and logic can go hand in hand in the form of adoption. I didn't give up on being her mother. I didn't decide not to love her anymore because of my choice in adoption. It was the depth of my love for her that gave me the courage to love her enough to let her go into another mother's arms.

After my decision of adoption, things quickly fell into place and God confirmed His plan with His fingerprints along the way. I remember driving down the highway with my adoption social worker with three waiting adoptive couple profiles. I flipped open the cover of the first photo album and admired the family. I remember a picture of them sitting in front of a Christmas tree, the mom with long hair and the dad beside her, with their dog posed nearby. They reminded me of my dad and stepmom when I was younger, we even had the same type of dog. The next picture was of a little blond-headed boy standing on the couch with their dog, looking out the window waiting for their daddy to come home. She would have a big brother! Being an only child most of my life, it was important for me that she have a sibling. I did look at the other two profiles, but it really was only this one that spoke to my heart. I had a feeling they were the family for my daughter.

We arranged a meeting about a week later at our social worker's office. I came with a whole list of questions to ask, everything from what kind of church they go to, to how they discipline, their work schedules, and extended family nearby to be involved in their lives. I arrived first and was sitting on one couch with all my parents beside me. Eventually they walked in with their son. We were both incredibly nervous, I'm sure. Their three-year-old son helped ease our way into conversations because he wasn't shy at all. He walked right up to me and stole the flip flops I had taken off to be more comfortable! In all my grilling questions, their honesty and love for each other and their child was obvious. Most things they said aligned with how I would have wanted to parent, if I could have. One huge topic, of course, was how we envisioned our adoption over the years. I only wanted an open adoption—one where I could visit, she would know who I was. I knew I needed that contact for my healing and for her to *see* how much I love her as she grew, so she would never question my love for her or why I chose adoption. Her dad had the best response to open adoption, "You are an important piece to her puzzle."

Later when they were told that we were officially matched, there was just one problem. I had already chosen a name...and so had they. I had been calling her a name for months since I had wanted to parent then. I really wanted to keep this name because it was a connection to me and my family. Here was another fingerprint from God—the name they had already chosen was almost the same as I had picked! I did tell them that if they let the first name stay, that they could pick the middle name. Without knowing the middle name I had chosen, they picked the same one! There were so many signs like this that reaffirmed over and over that they were the right ones for my daughter. We had several visits and many emails in the last two months of my pregnancy to get to know each other and our extended families more. We lived hours away from each other, but I let them know the update after every appointment and shared ultrasound pictures. They made me feel so welcomed into their family. It was clear that our bond wasn't just about the baby I was carrying, but included me as well.

My family continued to support me in my decision as well, they even bought two little puppies to help me emotionally heal and have something to nurture after my daughter was in her new home. They also threw me a "Leah Shower" since I wouldn't have a baby shower to celebrate. It was a touching way to honor my adoption decision and they gave me lots of things to pamper myself after the hospital.

In June 2004, I was set up for an induction on her due date so that it would be easier to make sure everyone could travel there for her arrival. While I didn't want them in the room, I wanted them nearby to meet her as soon as I was ready after birth. While I was in labor they went to the mall nearby to buy the nursery bedding I had picked out, yet another touch of their love for me and wanting me to be involved in her life. She was born at 9:00pm on the dot and I remember holding her, unable to speak with all the emotions washing over me and thinking, "I love you" over and over. When I could finally speak, the first words I told my parents were, "She is meant to be theirs," and the peace remained that I was doing the best thing for us.

After some bonding time and getting cleaned up, I invited

them in to meet their new baby girl. The image of her new dad cradling her in his arms with a single tear streaming down his face will forever be in my memory. As I watched him fall in love with her, I was so grateful that she would have a dad who adored her and would always be there for her. That was something I couldn't have provided for her, no matter how much money or support I might have had. The next day I cherished every moment with her. I changed diapers, I fed her bottles, and we took naps together hand in hand.

Before signing the adoption papers, her new parents sat down across from me said, "Are you SURE this is what you want? If you don't want to do this, you don't have to. We would be sad, but we will be okay." Their heart and compassion for me was so touching and assured me once again that this was the right thing to do for us. It meant a lot that they cared about me as much as they did about this new baby girl.

My new best friend, a birth mother I had met online, also arrived from her thirteen-hour drive to be by my side. She had placed nine months before, and her open adoption was a beautiful example of what I hoped ours would be. It meant so much to me to have her beside me when I signed the relinquishment papers, simply to have someone in the room who knew at the core how much pain I was feeling and having to push through to do what was best as I signed my shaky name.

Before we were released, we had a celebration in the hospital room. Tons of my family and friends arrived, baby gifts were given to her family, and kind words were said. I gave her adoptive mom a heart with her initials on it, and our daughter's on the back. I had one matching with my initials, and our daughter had one with both of her moms' initials. It symbolized our open adoption to me—how she had two moms who love her so much and would always be in her life.

Saying goodbye was hard, of course. We took pictures before we left and I had a smile on my face in them because I still felt at peace and joyful that I had brought this beautiful baby girl into the world, but I knew I would miss her. Driving away with an empty back seat and empty belly was such a loss, I felt empty. I cried and held my puppies. I wrote to her in a notebook her parents had given me. I called my best friend who would listen to me cry and simply say, "I know."

When she was a week old we had our first visit. I really needed to hold her again and her parents were so understanding. After that we had visits almost monthly for the first two years of her life. I would spend school breaks with them staying the night and even babysitting. I was honored when her mom would save some "firsts" for me, like feeding her solids for the first time and printing every picture possible for me to watch her grow in between visits. Even as a baby, the bond we had in my tummy felt so tangible. It was like she still knew who I was at visits, she would smile when I arrived and would fall asleep on me sometimes.

Twelve years down this adoption road, I'm constantly thankful for her family and amazed at how our story has ended up. We have visits several times a year, even sleepovers at my house now, and use technology in between visits to stay in touch.

I have been included in every birthday party, we have our own Christmas traditions, and feel like one giant extended family when we all visit.

Because of adoption, I was able to finish high school and college. I was able to find the love of my life and start a family of my own. I now am a freelance writer for a few popular mom blogs, along with working on a book of our story and advocating what open adoption can be. Unlike the old adoption days, I am here to be a piece in her puzzle of life. She knows I am her birth mom and adoption is her normal. It isn't confusing to her because it has always been a part of her life. Just like I have two moms with a mom and a stepmom, she has her mom and her birth mom. She is old enough now to come to me to ask questions, so now I can help her to process her own feelings about adoption.

She knows that my kids are her siblings and they have an amazing bond as well. They share talents and interests that obviously come from my side. I love that her family embraces that about her, too. We all have a mutual respect for what we bring to the adoption table—I bring the roots and biology, they provide the nurturing and give her wings.

Open adoption gave us *both* a better chance at life and God knew that. He used this experience to draw me near to Him, to trust Him, and to redeem my life. God wrote our story for His glory and I love to watch it continue to unfold as she grows—it only gets better!

—Leah Outten

## Nineteen
## *Finding Solace*

I used natural family planning successfully for almost three years. It was during this time I started having physical symptoms of an aggressive latex allergy. I had a stressful work week with a new company and was one of three employees. I was asked to cover a co-worker's nine-to-twelve hour shifts about an hour before they started for two weeks in a row. This was the hardest I've worked in my young adult life.

I slipped on counting my ovulation days and ended up conceiving accidentally. The day I tested pregnant I felt like I fell down a well. I was only twenty-one and I knew it would be the death of many of my "friendships." You see, these people weren't my friends because they ditched me after I couldn't get drunk and do drugs with them. Some simply didn't agree with my decision to add one more human to our already overflowing population on earth, but hey, I'm not the single source of global warming, guys. They turned out to be really horrible friends if you ask me. I expected to lose some, but even the supportive friends canceled plans and eventually stopped calling altogether.

If it wasn't for a supportive partner, I don't think I would have had the courage to keep my pregnancy. He met every whim of despair and struggle with comforting hugs and promises to support our family. When I told my employer I was pregnant they told me, "You have twenty-eight more weeks to decide if you want to keep your position here." I've never felt my stomach drop like it did that day. My employer tried to convince me to quit, saying I could become a "welfare queen" and make more money than he does by "living off the government." I felt defeated, wounded, and I cried every time I was alone that day. I had terrible morning sickness throughout the beginning of my pregnancy. The hormones felt like the strongest PMS I'd ever experienced. Life felt like untied shoes and I was tripping onto asphalt. I cried for the life I thought I was losing and the dream job that turned into a nightmare of employment.

I thought about aborting at least once a day. My partner continually told me he supported whatever my decision was and that he loved me and was ready to have a family. He wanted me to know he would still love me through this no matter what happened. I had to take my two female puppies to get spayed the same week my boss coerced me to quit my dream job. We decided to attend a free clinic that day while they were away at surgery. I remember how tough it was to take them to get their reproductive organs chopped out after finding out I was pregnant. I can laugh about it now at twenty-eight weeks pregnant, but that day it just made me cry. Oh the hormones! I couldn't take them to the office, so I asked my partner to go for me. I had never thought so seriously about taking away reproductive rights of a puppy. What if they wanted to be mommies?

The first time I saw my daughter as a tiny peanut with an

even smaller fluttering heart it changed my life. Nothing would ever be the same. She was real and she was alive. We heard her heartbeat for the first time. I was at a loss for words and felt frozen in time. I felt water droplets on my neck before my partner collapsed into my shoulder with big, slow tears rolling down his cheeks. I looked up at him intently studying our baby, a soft trembling smile on his lips. The rest of the appointment was a sheer blur. We had lunch afterwards and he asked me, "Do you want to keep it?" Before he finished his sentence I blurted out an astounding, "YES!" I couldn't say no. I couldn't stop thinking about the what-ifs. What if I abort and something happens that makes me infertile? What if I try again ten years later and I cannot conceive? What if I never decide I'm ready for children and regret terminating this pregnancy? What if I waste away my twenties, thirties, and forties, with nothing to show for it? What if my partner dies far before I do and growing old becomes lonely? I knew that accepting my pregnancy and choosing to carry my daughter for the next nine months would be the most challenging and rewarding feat I'd ever experienced. I knew that even though I was afraid it was the best thing for me. Pregnancy was a challenge to step outside my comfort zone. This challenge allowed growth in so many ways and allowed me to learn the depths of exhaustion, love, patience and perseverance. I knew in that moment my life changed forever. I'm thankful every day for my decision to keep her.

My first daughter is due in early June. I chose to name her Solace. It means to find comfort or consolation in a time of distress or sadness. Solace offered me relief from my tumultuous twenties, a decade that is simply thrown away for so many individuals. Solace offered me comfort and enabled me to take control of my power as a woman. She inspired me to cheerfully step forward into motherhood. I wish nothing more than for her to know she may find solace in herself in times of need. That she need not seek to fill emptiness with outside substances. That she has everything she will ever need inside herself. I hope for her to find solace inside her heart, especially when I am no longer there to provide her with the solace of my embrace.

—Hannah Elizabeth Ball , Joshua Argüelles & Solace Esther Argüelles.

## Twenty
## *It Will All Be Okay in the End*

Many years ago, before I met and married my husband Jeff, I did one of the hardest things a woman can do by placing my four-day-old beautiful baby girl on the altar of God and into the arms of another mother. I knew in my pregnancy, during my last year of college, and after a battery of painful and sleepless nights that she was not mine to raise. So I thoughtfully and heartbreakingly created an adoption plan. This was before open adoption was really a thing, so her adoptive mom and I felt like pioneers. By the grace of God, I have always been a part of her life and she has always been a part of mine and my other five children's. Jeff loves her like one of his own. And the fact that I've adopted two children myself, later in life, has made my experience as a birth mom come full circle.

Today, I met her new baby boy, Tucker, who is technically my grandson. We're still pioneering many aspects of the open adoption process, still navigating our roles in each other's lives. I'm comforted by the beautiful life she's had, the great husband who loves her so dearly, and the strong and dedicated mother she's becoming. I feel more like her sister than her mom. I walked about her home and snapped photographs of family pictures on her wall and felt a peaceful assurance that we are in God's hands. And it will all be okay in the end.

—Cherie Burton

## Twenty-One
## *Two Boxes*

"Here, take these," she says to me, handing me two boxes. "I can't do it, it's too hard."

I take the two boxes out of her hands. She won't give me eye contact.

"Everything is in there—my journal, the ultrasound pictures, the adoption letters, pictures," and her voice trails off. I don't know what to say.

"What you're doing is really important," she says, encouraging me to continue in my research. What she doesn't realize is this has taken its toll on me. The first time I conducted a phone interviewed I cried until I had a headache, but collecting stories of unplanned pregnancy has opened my heart up in a way I never expected. . Yes, I feel pain, their pain and I may get angry or sad at the injustices many of them face, but I also feel their strength, even when they think they are weak. Those who are members of the "unplanned pregnancy" club are my new heroes. They are the strongest women I know.

"My kids don't know they have a fourteen-year-old brother. I've kept this quiet for so long."

She turns back to her car and opens the door.

"Thank you," I say, but what I really want to say is "I'm

in awe that you have trusted me with your heart and soul. I will reverently look through these boxes with love and respect. I will do my best to tell your story, to tell your son's story."

Once inside my home, I open the lid of the first box and see several ultrasound pictures. Underneath that is a newborn photo of a beautiful Asian baby, with spiked black hair. His little hands are beautiful and I can almost feel how soft his skin is. Newborn babies smell like the blossoms of an apricot tree and my senses pick up on the sweetness of him.

How did she do it? She placed him for adoption that very day, most likely just after this newborn photo was taken. I peer into the box and I see it underneath some loose papers—a photo of her holding her newborn son. She's wearing a hospital gown and lying in bed, holding her baby just as tight as she's holding back her tears. The pain in her face is unmistakable, like a scar that might never go away. Who took the photo? Perhaps her mother, a friend? They say a picture says a thousand words, and it would be impossible to write how she felt at this moment, knowing her son was soon to be placed with another.

I pick up the loose papers of her journal. She starts by writing how she used to be a good girl, but once she befriended the wrong crowd she started making choices that took her on a different path. Her self-esteem suffered, as did her relationship with her parents. She started college, but moved back home within a year. Because of her lifestyle, she couldn't keep up with work and school. She stayed with her boyfriend, whom she'd known since elementary school, for three years. When she became pregnant, she thought he'd marry her. Instead he said, "I don't think I really love you."

*I'm 22 and pregnant. To most people, this would be a very exciting time in their life. For me it has to be one of the hardest and saddest because I'm placing my baby for adoption.*

She turned back to her faith, back to her parents and back to what she knew to be true. When she first met with the social worker, she knew adoption was the right answer for her. A feeling as true as a flame burned through her when she saw a photo of the family that would soon adopt her son. What a gift to know with such certainty that these were the right people.

*I didn't just wake up one morning and decide to be immoral. It started way back in 10th grade when I tried my first cigarette. After that, one thing led to another and I ended up hanging out with the wrong crowd. Growing up, I didn't see my life this way and looking back, I can't believe I let it happen. I always wanted freedom, but I guess I allowed myself too much freedom.*

She is married now and a mother of four more beautiful children. I see her in the carpool line at school. Her family is exceptional, her children are darling and she smiles as she takes them into her arms. She is an athlete who works each day to be strong. I used to think strength came easy to her, but now I see how she's had to work for it. She doesn't know me very well, but she trusts me with this experience. She has given me two boxes full of memories of the child she had fourteen years ago. He is being raised by beautiful people, his hair is still spiked and he smiles just like his mom.

—written by Laura Lofgreen

# Twenty-Two
## *I Always Wondered What Happened to the Children I Aborted*

I grew up in a totally dysfunctional family. My grandma had ten kids and was very poor. She left my alcoholic grandfather and kept her first three children. My mother was the oldest and she gave the rest up for adoption, two at that time, then one by one, until the final two who were twins. One of them in the middle had died.

I started drinking alcohol at age twelve on the weekends, and by fifteen had crossed the line to an alcoholic and had no more choice. My agency was taken away by Satan. He had won. I started smoking cigarettes and pot as well. At fifteen, I became pregnant from a guy I had known just the one night. When I told my mom I was pregnant, and I knew a friend who had recently had an abortion, and she totally agreed that was the answer. I was pressured more than anything to get one because she was so angry with me for becoming pregnant. I have often wondered where these children who were aborted went.

Later I met a boy and fell in love. We were together a long time. He would give me black eyes, bloody noses, fat lips and once broke my jaw, which I told the hospital ER had been caused by someone's knee while messing around with a football at the park…all a big lie. Mark was his name and he eventually broke up with me due to my drinking leaving me devastated. We dated again for a short while when I was seventeen, at which time I became pregnant again. I so wanted to keep the baby, but knew my drinking had gone too far and was worried how the child would be born so I aborted again. I remember I had to go to another city because I was just over three months and that was the limit where I lived in Redding, CA. I asked to see it, and saw a tiny baby fully developed in a baby food jar, but mostly just a translucent hand and arm as the rest was murky. I cried a lot after I saw it and had wished Mark had wanted to keep it, too.

My first husband had several affairs and drug and alcohol issues and after our two daughters were born I finally divorced him and shortly thereafter started going to church. I'm not sure if there is a repentance process or what but due to me being so young and having my mother's encouragement to have those abortions, I hoped I could be forgiven. I never had an example of how to live a good life. I only recall a handful of memories of my real dad who was an alcoholic, now dead since 1999 at age sixty. One was him holding my mother down on the bed and punching her in the face and I can recall everything going in super slow motion.

I knew I wanted more children and loved being a mother. While married to my first husband, before I had any idea of ever divorcing, I had a dream three times about my future husband which I thought was odd, but it seemed more real than life itself.

I couldn't see his face, but knew I would know him by how he made me feel. I explained it as not being an earthly love, but far beyond. I needed to get out of my abusive marriage.

I developed anorexia and bulimia and after my divorce, I stopped having my period for three years. I wasn't remarried, but wanted to be and longed for more children. I went to a doctor who did everything he could to "jump start" my periods. I'd bleed for a day and be done. Finally he told me I'd never be able to have more children. I was devastated. I once had a prayer with a friend at church about helping me with my illness as I had many times. I felt that within just a few days I'd receive a wonderful gift from God. I already knew what it would be and within a week I started my period and was every twenty-eight days like clockwork for many, many years. Most women call it a curse but it truly is a wonderful gift designed to allow us to procreate and become mothers. Every time I started my period thereafter I would smile. I remarried and had four more children. They were all born through C-section and I almost died while delivering my last son, but God took care of me. My mind continued to wonder where the children I aborted were. I hope I have them with me now.

—Kim C.

## Twenty-Three
## *My Parents Were Determined to See Their Grandbaby Face to Face*

It was a cold winter night, just after Christmas, when I had a terrible situation in which I could not escape. As tears streamed down my face, I knew that my life would be altered forever, if I even could make it out alive. I did not even realize fully what was happening, I just knew that it was not good. After this crime of rape occurred, this grown man told me that I would never forget him, as he had taken my virginity, and because of that, I would always remember him.

After the sexual assault had taken place, I was told of how much money could be had, if I were to join his prostitution ring. Sitting there completely baffled, confused, shocked, bruised, bleeding, hurt; how do I answer this, especially being threatened of death, and that of my family's lives were on the line. I sat there, and believed that I had to be strong, my life in the matter of minutes had sculpted into something you see in the picture screens, and it was time for me to get with the program.

Since I already felt damaged and used how do I return to the teen girl I was before, who do I call for help, where do I go? I was terribly embarrassed, and did not want to make a big deal out this, partly because I felt it was my fault, I had believed his lie to a certain extent. And, I was so fearful of the court system, I knew that if I called the police, one day I would be on the witness stand being ridiculed, demeaned, and exploited.

Therefore, I committed myself towards this mission of joining the sex industry. I was severely damaged inside emotion wise. After the initial abuse, it took a few weeks to heal as far as the physical aspect of being beat, but the distress would linger for years. I feared sex, and felt that I needed to overcome it by putting myself in the same position. I thought I was facing my fears. As twisted as this sounds, my 13 year old brain was trying to cope with the circumstance all by myself.

What I have noticed throughout my life, many women who are raped, either goes two ways. They stay away from sex out of horror, or they dive into unhealthy sexual encounters trying to conquer the trauma. This is how I handled it, plummeting to the bottom, and what more chaos it added.

Multiple nights I would come home from a night as a prostitute, to find that my parents were up waiting for me. I had been caught red handed sneaking out of the house during late night hours again. Having to be very vague about everything, these late nights were translated as I was in utter rebellion. This only separated my parents and me into opposite ends of a boxing ring. And, so it was, this sent me further into relations with multiple men that I was sold to.

This was my nightly job, and during the day I was a full time student, and by afternoon I was an athlete. To say the least, I was exhausted! Night after night, for two long years I endured this, lack of sleep, black eyes, pregnancy scares, etc. Until one day, I could no longer tolerate this, I was at the end of my rope, and my body had given way. I did not care if I got hurt, or even murdered. I stopped showing for pick-ups at our normal stops.

Much to my surprise, my pimp let me go. Can you believe? He did not do anything that he had claimed. This was an answer to prayer. I ran scared for a while, but after a few months I could begin to relax and try to piece my very shattered life back together. I never spoke to him again, nor did I communicate with those individuals associated with him.

I began a new school, counting it a pleasure for a fresh start. I went through high school, graduating a year early and desiring to go into the medical field as a nurse. I was back on course for the most part, however, still struggling and carrying a heavy weight on my shoulders that never seemed to cease. My peers had no clue, but often wondered why I reacted, or acted in certain manners. One time, I did try to confide in a close friend, only for the topic to turn awkward and our relationship distanced.

After graduating, I quickly returned to my old ways. I was used to the structure of high school, and could not cope with the independence that came with adulthood. Drugs, sex, and rock in roll was my life, countered with my attempts to advance in life through education. However, that all came to a screeching halt when I found myself in a crisis pregnancy.

I was in heavy crisis mode, therefore on the phone I went to call our nation's largest abortion provider. I had covered all of the bases, ensuring that no one could hear me making this telephone call. I knew that my Christian parents would not approve, and I could not see carrying this child to term not even knowing who his father was. I had to be tough, I had to block off any feelings of connection that would arise between my unborn baby and me. What I ended up doing was tapping back into the loneliness that the streets brought. I was on my own in dealing with this, or so I thought.

During this phone conversation with the abortion facility, somehow or another, my father overheard me, so he opened the door, and said these words, "Are you pregnant." And, very arrogantly, I responded, "Yea, why?"

My father was silent; he turned and quietly closed the door, as I remained on my bedroom's floor, with one hand holding the phone's receiver to my ear. I wondered what his plan of action would be, you know, the usual, would he kick me out, or yell at me? None of that occurred at all. In fact, it was the exact opposite. Over the next couple of weeks, he demonstrated unconditional enduring love to me. He would awake early in the morning to cook me breakfast, warm my car, make sure I had what I needed for college that day, and ask me how I was doing - Though he never specifically asked about the pregnancy, that is what he was referring to.

I was blown away by his sweet love. My father stands 6 foot 6 inches, and fought in war as a Marine, suffering from post traumatic stress disorder. My mother did her very best to keep our family of five together, working two jobs, and stressed beyond belief. During my whole life, our family had its share of hectic conditions, but I am so thankful to God that my parents had a relationship with Christ, or else no telling what would have come to pass for myself.

One night, we were sitting down together for dinner. I had come to the conclusion that it was going to be over soon, the abortion was fast approaching. There was a false sense of aspiration, I could smile, but deep down I was already grieving the future loss of my child. However, I was not going to admit that.

Everyone at the table began talking about the baby. What was transpiring? The very first time that this little one was being called a life, a child, a human! I sat there taken off guard; I was stunned, not knowing what to say. *I have already made up my mind; please do not try to alter my conclusion,* I thought. But, for three hours of high intensity, my mom talked, cried, negotiated, and begged me not to abort this precious one. As I sat there unable to hold the weeping inside, when I came up with a concern, my mom was quick to meet that need. However this pregnancy looked, she was determined to see her grandbaby face to face.

And so it was, I agreed, we were going to have a baby! Over the next several months, my parents were my inclusive support system, no matter what came about, they were always there. They defended me on all fronts, including those in our church who did not have my best interest at heart.

Months later, a nine pound two ounce bouncing baby boy was born! My mother never left my side for a moment during labor, and soon after delivery, my father entered the room with a huge smile across his face letting me know how beautiful he was, with all ten fingers and ten toes. Before I knew it, we were celebrating his first birthday!

I went on to marry my child's father, whom I met when I was 18 years of age. Now married many years later, we have two other children together, so totaling three. We endured self made hardships for a long time; the old addictions but adding jail time, marital cheating, gambling, etc. Consequently, after I almost committed suicide, we walked into a church, and gave our lives over completely to the Lord. In the course of this time frame, I spent much time on my face before the Lord, shedding tears, as He was mending my heart. Seven months later, my husband and I were headed off to Bible college full time. Throughout our time there, the Lord reconciled our marriage, healed our family and blessed us with a ministry assisting those in crisis pregnancies.

Though my life has been extremely difficult, it is now amazingly beautiful, because of Jesus. The Lord has given me back the years, and now I have joy and peace. Because of our repentance to Him, He graces us with His forgiveness, mercy, and freedom to be whole and live for Him. And, to think, this is available to all, pretty incredible. He is no respecter of persons; He desires a relationship with you. Call out to Him!

*At this time please allow me to envision a young child – let's say, a six year old little boy. Each year on this child's birthday, he gets super excited! And as a parent, as we are tucking him in bed at night, and though his birthday has not arrived yet, already he is telling you all about it. Each day thereafter, he reminds us as to how many days are left before his Big Day.*

*All parents usually own different kinds of keepsakes of their baby's birth – they may be pictures, a created baby book, or specially preserved baby clothes. Nonetheless, some things are saved reflecting memories of those wonderful life changing years – meaning that we are invested completely into this precious baby's life.*

*And as this child grows, he will want to see all of these things that were kept from his early years. We will tell him stories of when we found out he was on the way, and we will tell him of the day he was born, his first words, and his first steps, will all be shared. As this child hears these priceless remembrances, there will be a huge smile on his face. Do you know why?*

*Simply because we are telling him that he is legendary! When he was born he was so treasured his parents collected mementos just about him. Each year on his birthday, you are reminding him that not only once was he cherished as a baby, but he is esteemed and exceptional each year thereafter for as long as he lives!*

*Every child in this world deserves this same life's celebration – and even greater are the ones yet to be born. We still have time to make their earthly welcome be the best birthday they will ever have!*

*Will you help me in this? Please spread the word that for all – with no exceptions – new life is to be protected and received as a gift from God. Amen and Amen.*

—Dawn Guevara

## Twenty-Four
### *We Made It*

I'm forty-three years old and have a twenty-six-year-old son. Usually when the topic of kids comes up in conversation with people I have just met and I mention having a 26-year old, I can see someone trying to mentally calculate how old I must have been when I had my child. I typically get comments like, "You look way too young to have a child that old," or, "wow, I would have never thought you could have a child that old." These are mostly accompanied by looks of shock and disbelief. Some people try to clarify, "Oh, your stepson?" Rarely does someone straight up ask how old I am, but that happens, too. I have learned to use standby statements like, "I started a little early with him," or, "I'm lucky that my parents passed on really good genes."

It's hard to know where to begin this story because it could go back so far. Let's start when I left home shortly after my sixteenth birthday. The whys behind this are so many, and the events leading up to this point were destructive to my family and myself. To summarize, I grew up in a very religious family, and my very strong personality felt the need to rebel against this to the point where I could no longer live under their rules and had too much pride turn back. I left home one day with literally the clothes on my back.

After a few weeks of overstaying my welcome at friends' houses, I moved in with my most recent older boyfriend (he was nineteen). We moved into our first apartment with another couple as roommates on a ninety-nine dollar move-in special. My boyfriend was kind and sweet and made me feel safe. He took care of me. He had long dark hair and big deep brown eyes framed with the longest lashes. He had this way of smiling at me that made me melt. He was funny and brave—he wasn't afraid of anything—and he had a rough past. His mom and dad divorced when he was young and they both remarried. His dad had two sons with his new wife, and his mom had a daughter with her new husband. He felt that he didn't belong anywhere. As an early teenager he was wild and got mixed up with drugs, alcohol, and the law. We originally met a year before in a drug rehab program (but that is another story).

We were soon evicted from that apartment because no one was paying rent or probably any bills. As couples, we went our separate ways and my boyfriend and I rented another apartment a little way up the road on another ninety-nine dollar move-in special. We had nothing. My boyfriend worked at a car wash. I worked as a telemarketer for a carpet cleaning company. Money was tight, very tight, and the source of many arguments. We didn't have a car, so we walked or rode the bus everywhere. I remember always scrounging for change for the bus fare. We paid every bill in money orders purchased at the convenience store across the street and always paid in part with the large pile of change my boyfriend regularly swiped from car consoles at his job. Our apartment included cast-off furniture and a waterbed someone gave us for free. We rented a small nineteen-inch TV from Rent-a-Center. We were playing house and living probably like we would have in college—lots of partying, crazy friends, late nights, and a generally unhealthy lifestyle.

I remember the moment I learned I was pregnant. My life was so chaotic at that point that I didn't even realize that my period was long overdue. I wasn't trying to get pregnant, but I wasn't trying to not get pregnant. I started questioning the timing of my last period and my friend, who was just a couple of years older than me but already had her own baby, made a quick trip to the convenience store to steal a pregnancy test.

I remember sitting on the floor of the bathroom holding the pregnancy test in my hand, looking at the two blue lines and the instructions. Reading and re-reading the instructions to make sure I was looking at it right. I was stunned. Some people say their life flashes before their eyes in a near death experience. At that moment in time my future with this child flashed before my eyes. Mostly, the environment I didn't want this baby to grow up in. We lived in a cheap and shady part of town. Our apartment complex was timeworn and dirty. The grounds were dusty, with more dirt than patchy grass and a lot of pet waste. Many areas were in need of repair—peeling paint, broken window screens, broken playground equipment. We had neighbors who bragged about trading crystal meth for diapers at the convenience store across the street. Another neighbor's apartment was a complete disaster—she had two children and someone must have called

Child Protective Services because there was a social worker hovering around for several days. Mostly the children in the complex just never seemed clean. They wore mostly grungy, ill-fitting clothes, or just a too-big t-shirt and diaper. The bottoms of their feet were permanently black from walking barefoot in the dirt. They had dirt in the creases of their neck and elbows. Their parents let them stay out in the common areas way too late—they seemed like feral cats roaming the complex. The strange contrast was that most of these people were kind and wouldn't hurt anyone. They just didn't know a life any different. Growing up in an upper middle-class family, I did. More than anything, I was determined to not be a teenage pregnancy statistic.

I knew I could do it. I knew people who were already doing it—young girls who already had a baby on their hip. And if they could do it, so could I. My boyfriend really didn't have much to say other than mentioning we had "options," but to me there was only one option – keeping this baby. I didn't think I could stand to know that I had a child out in the world who thought I gave up on him. And in my mind at the time, abortion wasn't even a consideration. Friends were quick to provide advice and recommended applying for state assistance—AHCCSS for medical care, food stamps, WIC for supplemental nutrition. There were different programs for state funding assistance as well. The next week I took a bus to the Department of Economic Security, known by most as DES. I stood in line for what seemed like hours, to end up with a stack of paperwork to complete (no computer applications back then). My friends coached me on what to say at my social worker appointment. I would say I was going to be a single mom without support, that my parents were no longer supporting me, so I would get the maximum amount of support. In a few days I was sitting in the DES office for my appointment with a social worker. It was a surreal moment. How had I gotten to this point? Never in my young dreams did I ever consider at some point in my life I would be applying for welfare. Little did I know this was the start of building courage. This would be the first of many lessons of the importance of tenacity and the importance of advocating for myself and this baby.

After getting state assistance in order, it was time for me to get back in contact with my parents and family. I didn't want to go to them in a crisis, I wanted to go to them with a plan. I wanted to show them I was an adult and had this covered. And I didn't need their help. However, I did need something from them - a notarized signature that would allow me to get married. I met my mom at a McDonald's and it was the first time I had seen her or talked with her in months. When I asked what she thought when I asked to meet with her she said she figured I was either pregnant or wanted to get married. My answer to that was both. I feel like my family took this turn of events surprisingly in stride. I think what I had put them through up until this point had probably numbed them and they were always waiting for the next shoe to drop.

We started to rebuild our relationship, and my mom encouraged me to consider going back to school. I had dropped out of high school when I left home. Going back to high school was not an option, so I started looking through the phone book for schools. I found a for-profit school that was on our bus route. It was located on the upper floor of a mall and didn't look very school-ish. The admissions office recommended I complete my GED first, which I did, easily. I remember thinking, if that is all I needed to know to get a high school diploma I was glad I didn't waste the time. Soon thereafter, thanks to a Pell grant and student loans, I was enrolled in the General Business Certificate program. I loved school. It made me feel smart and like I was accomplishing something, not only for myself, but for my baby's future.

While I was working to better myself and improve our future, my boyfriend seemed to be heading in the opposite direction. He had always drunk alcohol, smoked marijuana regularly, and would partake in pretty much any drug that was available in the moment. I wasn't an angel myself, by any means, but at the moment I found out I was pregnant I knew things would have to change. He was changing, but in a different way and the situation seemed to be amplifying. He was drinking more, much more. He was being reckless. From the beginning, I knew my boyfriend had a very short temper. It was scary at times but other times made me feel safe. It would come out mostly when he had been drinking but sometimes for no reason. I recall one time he was frying two eggs on the stove. He flipped an egg over and the yolk broke. In a split second he erupted in rage, turned and punched a hole in the drywall. Another time when he had a drinking glass in his hand, something set him off and he hurled it at the wall with such great force it exploded and shattered in a million pieces. Early in our relationship his anger wasn't directed at me, but shortly after I found out I was pregnant, this began to change. It started with small things that looking back should have been big warning flags. One time he got angry for some reason when I wasn't home. When I returned, I saw he had smashed a chia pet I had grown on our back patio for several weeks. As I said, money was tight, so spending money on something as frivolous as a chia pet was elating. He knew I loved that dumb chia pet. I had a cat that I also loved dearly, named Spidy. My boyfriend would erupt in rage and pick up my cat like he was going to hurt him, his face twisted with gritted teeth. It was only after my hysterics and begging would he drop him on the floor and walk away. His abuse toward me started with small things. He would shove me against the wall and scream in my face. He would grab my wrists and twist them and twist my arm behind my back until I cried in pain. When this happened his face was so distorted—like he was a completely different person. I learned to walk on eggshells around him, trying desperately not to trigger any anger. But no matter how hard I tried, something, even the most ridiculous thing, like one of his male friends talking with me longer than he thought they should, would bring consequences. I became afraid and felt a constant surge of adrenaline as an undertow—like an endless fight or flight reflex wound tight as a spring. It was exhausting. I flinched when he would make a quick move around me. I know people saw this and now wonder what they thought. There was only one instance when someone in our circle of friends raised concern. We were at a friend's house and he again erupted with anger towards me. He didn't touch me that time, but I know it was clear I was scared he would. When everyone left the room one of his friends stayed behind and asked me with such sincerity, "Are you OK?" I knew he wasn't just asking about that instance. He knew there was a bigger picture. I nodded "Yes" as tears silently slid down my face. So many things during this time of my life are murky and clouded; however, I have a perfect memory of this moment. I was sitting on a mattress on the floor and he was standing in the doorway. There was a colorful silk tapestry in earth tones hanging on the wall and a fish tank on the dresser. I knew in that split second if I had answered differently it could have changed the trajectory of my life. But I didn't.

At this point the question becomes why didn't I leave? Why didn't I call my parents and tell them I needed help? Why didn't I reach out in any way? The conflict was that after every instance of rage, he was so kind, completely attentive and loving, so apologetic. He would buy me small gifts. He blamed it on the alcohol, blamed it on the stress of money, blamed it on his upbringing (once he started getting physical with me I found out that his father had been abusive toward his mother) but mostly blamed it on me. I "made" him do it. I justified it in my head that my baby needed his father and he wasn't actually hitting me. We needed to be a family. He needed me. Sure I had bruises on my arms and wrists, bruises where he would grab and pull the skin on my back, knots on the back of my head where he slammed my head against the wall. But I didn't have black eyes or broken bones or blood —that's what you see on TV as abuse. That changed one night.

It was the night before Easter in 1991 and we had plans to go to his grandmother's house the next day. His father, stepmother, and half-brothers were going to pick us up Sunday morning. I wish I could recall what set him off in this particular instance, but I don't. I just know it escalated quickly. It started with the shoving and what I came to think as manhandling. I had learned to curl up in a ball to protect my stomach and tuck my arms in so he wouldn't grab them and try to drag me into a different room. I was starting to panic because I could tell he was out of control. He pushed me back against the wall, grabbed my chin forcing me to look at him, and then spit in my face. I broke free and was cowering on the couch. The phone was next to the couch and I picked it up—it was an old-style rotary phone. To call who? I have no idea. The police? My parents? His parents? When I picked up the phone handset he went ballistic. He reached to press the hang-up button on the phone base, but instead picked it up and swung it full force, directly across my face. I remember an explosion of pain and realizing what people meant by "seeing stars" when they hit their head. I had never been hit in the face, by anyone. My nose exploded in blood. I had never even had a bloody nose. My boyfriend looked at me with the phone base still in his hand, handset on the floor, stunned. I don't know how many seconds passed, but I could only feel my heart pounding out of my chest and my face throbbing, my nose dripping blood. He turned and threw the phone into the wall with such strength that it stuck in the drywall. This turned into what I can only describe as psychotic blind rage and he began kicking and punching holes in the walls of the living room. He punched multiple holes through multiple walls throughout the room. Big holes that he would punch and kick multiple times to make even bigger. He kicked the wall in the living room so hard his foot went through the wall into the kitchen and it pushed the stove into the middle of the floor. I ran to the bathroom in our bedroom while this was happening to grab something to clean up my face and locked the bedroom door. I crawled into bed, sobbing. What have I gotten myself into? I felt stuck. I had nowhere to go. At that point I was close to eight months pregnant—who would hire me? And even if I could get a job, I could only work part time because I was still going to school. I had no money. Just last week I stood in the drug store for fifteen minutes deciding if it was worth spending forty cents on a tube of lip balm. And then what happens when the baby comes? I sobbed in despair and felt so helpless. I was so angry for getting myself into this situation, and feeling so selfish that I now was bringing a baby into this picture. Surely he will change with the baby comes, I thought. He doesn't mean it. He had a rough upbringing and doesn't know how to manage his emotions. There was silence in the other room and that frightened me. Soon, I heard the doorknob try to turn. It was still locked. He started knocking calmly on the door asking to let him in. He was sorry. I could tell he was crying. So what did I do? I got up and unlocked the door. He wrapped his arms around me and just said, "I'm so sorry" over and over and over and over. We spent the night like that—with his arms wrapped around me holding tightly and both crying. The next thing I knew it was light outside, and I heard knocks on the front door. His family was there to pick us up. I jumped up and ran into the bathroom to look at my face. I had an excruciating headache. There was a large bruise on my cheek, nose and under one eye. There was still blood crusted under my nose. I peeked out of our bedroom door and saw the living room was a disaster – holes in every wall, dry wall pieces and dust everywhere. Chairs overturned. I knew I couldn't answer the door. They knocked and knocked and knocked. They had to know we were in there. I sat on the nubby, itchy couch and silently cried.

This event was a turning point. I knew I needed to take action, if not for myself, for this baby. I am not a religious person, but I do believe that everything happens for a reason. The next events that unfolded in my life were surely the universe telling me what I needed to do.

A few weeks prior to this episode I had applied for a part-time cashier job I found in the newspaper want ads for an auto paint store. Even though I was almost seven months pregnant at the time, you really couldn't tell if I wore baggy clothes. And we needed the money. I ended up getting the job and showed up for the first day of training in a baggy hooded sweatshirt. There were several others who were starting in different positions the same day. As the day unfolded, the person training us made a comment about recently having a baby. She explained that while she was pregnant she had to wear a special mask if she entered any of the painting garages. I raised my hand and said that I would need to have access to one of those masks, since I was pregnant. The trainer looked at me for a moment with a confused look on her face, but went on. Before breaking for lunch she asked for everyone's drivers licenses to make copies. I had to admit that I didn't have one. I was seventeen and due to my history, my parents had never agreed to sign to let me get my license. After the lunch break she came back to me and said, "I'm sorry, but you can't work here if you are pregnant." I was confused. She had just told us that she had worked there while pregnant with accommodations—and I reminded her of this. She said, "Well, you don't have a license either and you have to have a driver's license to work here." But I wasn't a delivery driver like some of the others in the training class; I was going to be a cashier. She made it clear that I should leave. I was stunned and embarrassed, and walked to the bus stop in front of the store. I held myself together until I stepped on the bus and then fell apart sobbing. This was supposed to be a new start, I would be making my own money, and it was a step toward a new life. I rolled this around in my head and realized that what this trainer had said to me was likely illegal. I knew a little about this because my grandmother had been an equal opportunity manager for the government for many years. I had heard many stories about her cases and she had a long history of fighting for women's rights. And then I was angry. I called my grandma when I returned to my apartment and explained to her what had happened. She was even angrier than I was. She wanted me to immediately contact the local EEOC office and file a discrimination complaint, which I did. A few weeks later, with my grandma as the mediator, a settlement was negotiated with the auto-paint store for an award of $3000. As this was playing out, I knew this was my chance. It would have taken months and probably years for me to save up enough money to make it on my own. With this settlement, I could start a new life.

My boyfriend knew this settlement was coming and was constantly asking about the status. I started secretly looking for another place to live while he was at work. I was just a couple of weeks from my due date. I told my mom I needed to leave my boyfriend, but I don't think I told her why. She knew he was abusing alcohol and drugs, and that might have been all she needed to know. I found an ad in the newspaper for a basement apartment. The rent was cheap, but it was in a better part of town. When I arrived to meet with the landlord I learned it was an older woman who was renting the basement of her home. Before her husband passed away, he had remodeled the basement to make it an apartment so his wife would have a source of income. Her name was Lavina and she loved cats. There were many cats that lived in the home, and even more that she fed outside. But the apartment was perfect—a furnished one-bedroom with a small kitchen, bathroom, and living area, and gold shag carpeting throughout. At this point I was still receiving state assistance and after some calculations I determined I could stretch the settlement money until I graduated. One of the highlights of the general business program was the opportunity for job placement following graduation. If everything worked out, the timing would be perfect.

Now I had to figure out how to leave. I had already planned to leave most everything behind other than my clothes and the small amount of baby supplies I had gathered from garage sales. I asked my parents to be on standby to bring my dad's truck to my apartment so we could move everything in one trip. I knew I had to plan this when my boyfriend was not home or it would be a traumatic scene. I waited until he left for an evening shift at his Pizza Hut job, and then my parents came over. We started quickly loading the truck. Once I realized the gravity of what I was doing I started sobbing, shaking uncontrollably, and hyperventilating. I had cried so, so many tears over the last year, many times I thought surely I didn't have any more tears to cry. But in this instance I was so devastated, so scared, and so hysterical, that I cried harder than I ever had so far in my life. But I knew deep down I needed to do this and pressed forward. It was just one week before my May 13th due date.

I spent the next three days in my new lonely apartment crying and questioning everything I was doing. Was it the right thing? My throat was raw, my eyes swollen shut, and I couldn't stop shaking. I sat on that shag carpeting with my head in my hands for hours at a time. And then, I started having contractions.

Being a voracious reader throughout my life, I had read every pregnancy book I could get my hands on. Between that information and what my doctor told me, I was almost certain—although still pretty far apart—they were contractions. I happened to have a doctor's appointment that day and had already figured out a new bus route from the apartment. However, I was nervous about potentially being in labor and called my mom, asking if she could drive me to my appointment. While I was waiting for her, I went to the bathroom and saw mucus blood—what I knew had to be what my books called the "bloody show." This was real. This was happening.

The doctor examined me and confirmed it—I was three centimeters dilated. He told me to head to the hospital. I sat in my mom's car, stone-faced as she drove to the hospital. Suddenly, I erupted in emotion and explained to her the real reason I left my boyfriend—the abuse and not wanting to bring up my baby in that environment. Strangely, I don't remember her reaction.

My mom and dad were with me in the room for the labor and delivery. I arrived at the hospital at 12:00pm and my son was born at 10:30pm. It was May 9th, three days before Mother's Day. At this point I had not had any contact with my ex-boyfriend since I had left him three days before; however, he found out through friends that I was in the hospital. He showed up shortly after my son was born. This is another point that is murky in my mind. I don't remember how long he stayed, or where we left things when he left that night.

I stayed in the hospital for another day and had to meet with a social worker before leaving. She asked many questions and seemed skeptical about my ability to take care of this baby and what my plans were moving forward. I was only seventeen, after all. I could tell she was surprised that I seemed to have everything in order and was prepared to take this baby home.

I stayed with my family for two weeks so my mom could help with the baby, and then went back to my apartment. It was a very emotional and confusing time, and I considered multiple times reconciling with my now ex-boyfriend. But I found the longer I was away, the stronger I felt. And the more determined I was to think with a clear head and my baby's best interests in mind. Two weeks later I started looking for a day care because I needed to return for the next session of school. There was another state assistance program that would pay for his daycare while I was going to school. I still didn't have a car or driver's license so I needed to be strategic in finding a day care on the bus route and then a bus route to work with my school schedule. I found a day care that I liked and they agreed my son could start attending at five weeks old instead of the preferred six weeks old.

My typical day would be waking up, feeding my son and getting him ready, then putting him in a bouncy chair in the bathroom while getting myself ready. I would pack his diaper bag and my backpack and we would head out. We would catch the bus up the street, heading east. I would get off at the stop across the street from the day care, run across the street to drop him off, and then run back out to the bus stop on the day care side of the street to catch the bus that had turned around a couple of miles up and was now heading west towards school. I would spend the morning at school, and then take the bus back to his daycare in the late afternoon. Eventually the day care hired me to work there in the afternoons.

I had worked hard to make the settlement money stretch

as far as possible. I subsisted mostly on frozen meals and ramen noodles. And as I started making a small income from my part-time job at the daycare, my state assistance started decreasing. I was scheduled to graduate from my program in February and started working with a job placement associate at the school. It was getting to a critical point and I needed a real job.

My job placement associate got me an interview with a large financial company opening a new center in the area. I was eighteen years old, walking into a large corporation with zero on-the-job office experience. I had borrowed a suit and shoes from my mom, I think. I interviewed with multiple people that day and remembered thinking this was so out of my league and I would never get the job. I stayed positive, and tried to portray confidence, but left discouraged. I sent a follow-up thank you note as I learned from school and called a few days later to check in. I don't remember why, but I was taking a call from the company at the daycare where I was working. They were calling me to offer me the job. My title would be Secretary II, my salary $16,500. I felt like I was a millionaire. My knees went weak and I slid down the wall to be sitting on the ground. This time I was crying tears of joy. We did it. We made it. And it was only the beginning.

I met my husband at that first job. He was ten years older and the first person I dated who was stable and a rock for me. He made me laugh – I felt like it had been a long time since I did so, uninhibited. He was a contributing member of society with a good job and committed to a better future. I learned this was what a true safe love feels like. He loved me and all my past and all my faults. But most importantly, he loved my son. We dated for four years before we got married and will celebrate our 21st anniversary in a couple of weeks. My ex-boyfriend's parental rights were severed without contest (he never responded to or showed up for any legal actions) and my husband adopted my son the first year we were married. He is the only father my son has ever known. He had been married previously and had a daughter from his first marriage so we made our own little family. My son's biological father continued in a downward spiral – he ended up addicted to opiods, a full blown alcoholic, and was in and out of jail with multiple arrests for things like burglary, DWI, criminal trespassing, drug possession, and domestic violence. When he was a baby I took my son one time to visit him in jail, which solidified my feeling that he couldn't be in our lives. It ended up being an unspoken mutual decision and he saw my son less times than I can count on one hand, and all before he turned one year old. He never paid a dime in child support. He never married and never had any more children. I am ashamed to admit that many times throughout the years I thought it would just be easier if he died. That it would be easier on my son if he didn't have to live with the fact that his biological father was still living, but was not a part of his life. Then the call came in 2011 – he had passed away just prior to his fortieth birthday. My son was in his sophomore year at college. The official cause from what I understand was heart failure; however, I am certain that his years of drug and alcohol abuse was the main contributor. What I want my son to know is that his biological father staying away and giving us a chance at a successful, productive life was the best gift he could have ever given us.

I lived my life in reverse. I had a baby, got married, and then got my college degree as an adult. For me, that was the right thing to do. If I wouldn't have had a baby so young, I would have continued to spiral out of control and who knows where my life would have ended up. If I would have held it together and gone to college after high school, I likely would have flunked out. Getting my degree as an adult was much more meaningful and applicable at that point in my life. Professionally I have been successful far beyond what I ever thought in my dreams I could accomplish – and was making a six figure salary before I turned forty. I attribute this to my early lessons in tenacity, resourceful creativity, and learning to never settle. As well my husband has been an incredible professional example for me and has been supportive of growing my career - always encouraging me that I could do more, that I had more to offer.

I write this anonymously only to protect my family - both immediate and extended, as well as my son's biological father's family as I hold no ill will toward them. I am proud with what I have accomplished in life, and would be humbled if my story helps someone be brave and believe they can make it too - a life for themselves and their baby.

—Anonymous

## *About the Author*

Laura Lofgreen has been married to her wonderful husband Derek for eighteen years and is the mother of six children, five boys and one daughter, all named after Arizona towns. Her blog www.mydeartrash.com has over a million views and she writes about finding value in things we as a society throw away. An avid thrift store shopper, Lofgreen made a living selling used clothing on eBay and eventually got into refinishing vintage furniture, but most meaningfully, she writes about how after being sexually abused she felt like trash. My Dear Trash is about finding the value in ourselves, our children, our loved ones and with God. She is the founder of the social media campaigns projectused.com, (#projectused) #babyyoureworthit and #momauthor. In her young adult historical fantasies, memoir or non-fiction work, she seeks out those who have faced abuse and overcome great obstacles. Through her work, she hopes to demonstrate each one of us is of great worth and infinite value. When not writing, taking care of kids or doing laundry, she loves making chocolate chip cookies and going on long walks, but not at the same time of course.

### *Would you like to submit your story?*

Laura Lofgreen continues to seek out stories of unplanned pregnancy and those who have overcome great obstacles. If you'd like to submit your story or be interviewed, contact her at lauralofgreen@gmail.com.

Other Books by Laura Lofgreen

*Starving Girl – A Memoir*

*The Memory Catcher*

Made in the USA
Columbia, SC
02 April 2021

35492750R00119